D0065302

THE LAYMAN'S BIBLE COMMENTARY

THE LAYMAN'S BIBLE COMMENTARY
IN TWENTY-FIVE VOLUMES

THE LAYMAN'S
BIBLE COMMENTARY

Balmer H. Kelly, *Editor*
Donald G. Miller   *Associate Editors*   Arnold B. Rhodes
Dwight M. Chalmers, *Editor, John Knox Press*

VOLUME 25

THE FIRST, SECOND, AND THIRD LETTERS OF
JOHN

THE LETTER OF
JUDE

THE
REVELATION TO JOHN

Julian Price Love

JOHN KNOX PRESS
ATLANTA, GEORGIA

10 9 8 7 6 5 4 3 2

Complete set: ISBN: 0-8042-3086-2
This volume: 0-8042-3085-4
Library of Congress Card Number: 59-10454
First paperback edition 1982
Printed in the United States of America
John Knox Press
Atlanta, Georgia 30365

PREFACE

The LAYMAN'S BIBLE COMMENTARY is based on the conviction that the Bible has the Word of good news for the whole world. The Bible is not the property of a special group. It is not even the property and concern of the Church alone. It is given to the Church for its own life but also to bring God's offer of life to all mankind—wherever there are ears to hear and hearts to respond.

It is this point of view which binds the separate parts of the LAYMAN'S BIBLE COMMENTARY into a unity. There are many volumes and many writers, coming from varied backgrounds, as is the case with the Bible itself. But also as with the Bible there is a unity of purpose and of faith. The purpose is to clarify the situations and language of the Bible that it may be more and more fully understood. The faith is that in the Bible there is essentially one Word, one message of salvation, one gospel.

The LAYMAN'S BIBLE COMMENTARY is designed to be a concise, non-technical guide for the layman in personal study of his own Bible. Therefore, no biblical text is printed along with the comment upon it. This commentary will have done its work precisely to the degree in which it moves its readers to take up the Bible for themselves.

The writers have used the Revised Standard Version of the Bible as their basic text. Occasionally they have differed from this translation. Where this is the case they have given their reasons. In the main, no attempt has been made either to justify the wording of the Revised Standard Version or to compare it with other translations.

The objective in this commentary is to provide the most helpful explanation of fundamental matters in simple, up-to-date terms. Exhaustive treatment of subjects has not been undertaken.

In our age knowledge of the Bible is perilously low. At the same time there are signs that many people are longing for help in getting such knowledge. Knowledge of and about the Bible is, of course, not enough. The grace of God and the work of the Holy Spirit are essential to the renewal of life through the Scriptures. It is in the happy confidence that the great hunger for the Word is a sign of God's grace already operating within men, and that the Spirit works most wonderfully where the Word is familiarly known, that this commentary has been written and published.

THE EDITORS AND
THE PUBLISHERS

THE FIRST LETTER OF

JOHN

INTRODUCTION

The Christian gospel must make its appeal in a world where
there are many opposing ways of life. These ways are essentially
the same in all ages, though their forms of expression differ from
time to time. Some men seem to be especially chosen of God to
pick out these "worldly" forms of living and distinguish them
clearly from Christian truth. Such a one was the author of the
First Letter of John, a man gifted with penetrating insight, abiding
loyalty to Christ, and willingness to contend against the corrupt
thinking and acting which he found in the Church. His letter is
a marvel of deep thought expressed in the simplest of language.

The Situation

Perhaps we may most easily follow this author if we first realize how closely our contemporary problems parallel his, for in
this way we shall see the eternal nature of the battle he is waging
for truth. In every age we face some form of the question, What
is there in life that is real and what only *seems* to be? Does it
actually matter, for example, if men live pure and honest lives?
What difference to other people does it make whether we love
them or not? And if we believe in God, especially as he is revealed in Jesus Christ, how does that actually change things?

Such questions are not new. They have recurred in one setting
or another throughout history. They all center in the contrast between what seems to be and what actually is. But contrasts are
often made at the wrong points. Christian Science, for instance,
teaches that sin and pain are not real; if you do not think them,
they do not actually exist. Yet Mrs. Eddy and her followers are
quick to distinguish between "spirit" and "matter." The "spiritual" is the only true being and the "material" is unreal and
untrue. Such distinctions are almost as old as philosophy itself.

They were actively taught in the days when this letter was written. Some of them went all the way back to certain interpretations of Plato, others found their source in Zoroastrian teaching in Persia and had become mixed with some elements of Greek philosophy.

All such teaching, whether from the first century of our Christian era or in vogue today, roots in the basic idea that the spiritual and the material must always be kept apart; that the spiritual is always good and the material always evil. Such a philosophy is what we call a "dualism"; that is, it divides all that is into two spheres, the spiritual and the material, and thinks of the one as good and real and the other as only evil and imaginary. In the days when this letter was written, those who held such views were called "Gnostics," that is, "knowers," just as "agnostics" would mean those who say they do not know. Fundamentally they were people of proud self-consciousness who despised others. It was they who "knew" because they were essentially spiritual in nature, while the rank and file of men were doomed to be materially minded and ignorant of the truth.

One would expect to find such ideas in a pagan world, but the occasion for the First Letter of John is that they had become firmly rooted in the Church itself. And it is not altogether strange that this should have been so. After all, "Gnosticism," as it was called, has a certain kinship with Christianity. We too have a dualism. We too believe that good and evil are to be sharply distinguished, and that evil is bound up in an unhealthy greediness for the material things of this world. We too believe that we "know" the Lord and therefore know the true meaning of life. We too believe that God himself has chosen us to know him. It is small wonder that the Gnostics found fertile soil in the Early Church and that in the second and third centuries a number of leading churchmen called themselves "Christian Gnostics."

But the error of such thinking is all the more dangerous because it is subtle. For true Christianity is both spiritual and material. The Christian has a healthy regard for his body, for food and shelter, for health and comfort. According to the Gospels, Jesus not only taught "Blessed are the poor in spirit" (Matt. 5:3) but also "Blessed are you poor" (Luke 6:20)—that is, you who are poor in this world's goods but who have the Kingdom of God within you. Jesus fed the hungry and healed the sick, and he did not minister to them by teaching them that their sufferings were imaginary but by dealing with these conditions as with things that are real.

The Gnostics who troubled the Early Church reached their worst extreme in the so-called "Docetists," a word which means "Seemists." These Docetists, when they got a foothold in the Christian Church itself, did not hesitate to teach that Jesus could not have been the spiritual Son of God and have had a real human body at the same time, since the body was material, and hence evil. He must have only "seemed" to be in a body. They taught that the moral distinctions between good and bad did not really make any difference; they only seemed to. What mattered was the conquering of the material by the spiritual. Thus they blurred the distinction between honesty and cheating, between purity and grossness, between graciousness and selfishness. They did this in either of two ways. Some of them said that since all matter was evil and they themselves were of the spirit, what they did could have no effect upon their souls. They could easily become gluttons and drunkards, for no amount of wallowing in the mire could affect the real spiritual essence of their lives. Others held that since all matter was evil, they must carefully avoid it, and so they became hermits in order to keep themselves from contact with the world. Many of the Docetists scoffed especially at the doctrine of Christian love. Why, after all, should we bother to love men? People do not actually need care and sympathy and affection; they only seem to.

The Message

Against all such emphasis the First Letter of John is a fiery polemic. The Apostles, it insists, did not preach a vapory, unreal Jesus, but one whom they had seen with their own eyes and handled with their own hands (1:1-3). They did not teach a God who was withdrawn and known only to a select few, but one whose very nature was light (1:5). This God was not a "form-idea"; as revealed in Christ he was the very source of life itself (5:11-12). His inner nature is love, and the very fact that he loves is both the source and the dynamic of our love to one another (4:8, 16, 19). Christ is to be completely identified with "the word of life" (1:1). He did not simply *seem* to die; his death was a very real expiation—a washing away of our sins so that we might have true life (2:2). He was sinless, and therefore it is his will that we shall be; it is not a matter of indifference whether we sin or do not sin (2:29). He gave his life because of the love of God for all men, and this is enough to make it necessary that we, too, should love all (3:16). In short, our Christian faith does have a dualism, but it is not the dualism that the Gnostics and especially the Docetic Gnostics have always had—the dualism between spirit and matter. We do not set them against each other; we believe that both are of God. But our dualism is moral: love as against hate, righteousness as against sin, truth as against falsehood.

This little letter deals trenchantly with sin. The author defines it as "lawlessness," that is, living without a controlling principle (3:4). The Christian confession acknowledges sin to be real (1:8-9), just as the experience of being cleansed from sin makes clear that Christ is really the Savior (1:7). The passionate insistence on the need of sinlessness, which we find in this letter, is a testimony to the true nature of the union of the believer with his Lord (3:9-10). But this demand is no cold formal law; it is rather the pleading command of him who loves. And so the Christian must distinguish between love of the world and love of God and his will, for love and goodness are ever interrelated (2:15-17). As someone has put it, "Righteousness is love in the imperative mood." So it is that when the writer is most deeply involved in his thought of good living he rises to the heights in his picture of real love. Christian love is active helpfulness meeting genuine human need (3:16-18). Moreover, love is closely associated with the belief that Jesus actually reveals the true nature of God. The greatest of all passages on Christian love (4:7-21) follows immediately upon a statement of the necessity of distinguishing between "the spirit of truth and the spirit of error"; the confession that the perfect Christ is humanly real serves as the test of truth or error.

Equally real to this author and essential to his view of the Christian life is the true doctrine of knowledge. The "Spirit of God" (4:2) is the source of all faith and knowledge. Assurance is the result of life spent in fellowship with God and with those who are of the Spirit of God (1:3; 5:7-10). If one would really overcome the world, he is to do it, not by retreating from it as some of the Docetists did, nor yet by indulging in its wrong, as others gloried in doing, but by living in that faith which the Spirit of God makes possible, the faith which gives the actual victory over "the world" (5:4-5).

First John and the Gospel According to John

The relation of such teachings to the total Christian message is not hard to see. Especially does any Bible reader note the similarity of First John to the Fourth Gospel. Nouns such as "love," "truth," "light," and "life" occur frequently in both, as do verbs such as "walk," "abide," "know," and "believe." The whole idea of the new birth from God underlies both. There is the same direct, simple style, the same sharp contrasts, the same belittling of the formal dualism of the Gnostics, and the same insistence on the moral dualisms of the Christian faith. Both writings use a small vocabulary and repeat their words and ideas time and again. Both are apparently quite simple, yet really very deep. In both of them Christ the Word is the center of God's revelation to the world. In both there is no relative position for the faith; everything is absolute. One is either born again or he is not; one either loves or he does not; he either abides in the truth or he lives a lie. The Letter, like the Gospel, often has passages of great beauty and winning warmth; but, also like the Gospel, it often presents harsh judgment in no uncertain terms. Both stress the test of belief in action. And in both the doctrine of "eternal life," not as only a future but also as a present possession, controls much of the thought.

Yet there are marked differences, too, between the Gospel and the Letters of John. The First Letter is not so dependent on the Old Testament as is the Gospel. It is the judgment that takes place in men's lives from day to day that the Gospel stresses; the Letter emphasizes the final judgment. In the Gospel the return of Christ is spiritualized and may be thought of as the coming of the Holy Spirit; in the Epistle there is the expectancy of the "last hour." In the Gospel there is frequent expression of salvation in terms of identification with Christ, abiding in him as the branch in the vine; in the Letter, Christ is presented as the "expiation" for sin. These are differences of emphasis that do not necessarily point to difference in authorship and certainly do not contain essential contradictions.

Both the Gospel and the First Letter of John find a background in the Jewish sectarianism of their day. While this is perhaps much more true of the Gospel than of the Letter, it is important in the Letter itself. The Old Testament had already contrasted righteousness with evil, loyalty with unbelief, love with hate. And the Judaism of his day, quite as well as the Christian fellowship, was prepared to do battle with corrupters of the message of the prophets.

This has become much clearer of late through the publication of some of the Dead Sea Scrolls. The Essene-like community, whose worship and organization and manner of living these documents reveal, was engaged in the same struggle with falsehood which is to be found in the writings of John. And they went about it in much the same sort of way. Such contrasts as "the spirit of truth and the spirit of error" (4:6); such expressions as "eternal life" (5:11); such ideas as not loving the world at the same time that we love men (2:15), cherishing the truth within the fellowship (2:19-21), the constant emphasis on love of the brethren (as in 2:10; 3:16), even the thought of God's "word" (1:1) —all these and others are spiritual weapons in the Jewish community at Qumran as well as in John's great letter.

The Author

Who was the early Christian who could write so searchingly and yet so directly about the meaning of life, who could touch the sensitivity of his own age and of ours as well? The letter itself bears no name and gives no clue except its style and habit of thought. Christian tradition has long held that this letter and the two shorter ones that follow it were from the hand of "John." To some this is "John the Presbyter," a leader of Asia Minor of whom some Early Church Fathers speak, but to most this is John the closest of all the Apostles to Christ, the one who leaned back upon him at the farewell supper and caught most deeply his word and mood. These are "catholic"—that is, "general"—letters, for they represent the realistic handling of the needs of the Church at large, probably toward the end of the first Christian century.

The First Letter of John is often referred to as a "wisdom" epistle, for, like James and parts of Proverbs, it stakes out its truth in little gems of teaching. It is spiral in form; that is, its thoughts, which recur in no regular pattern, gradually rise to the climax of love and true knowledge. Ideas progress in a series of "cycles," and the writer comes back to the same thought again and again that he may amplify it and show how it fits into all other parts of the truth he has been discussing. The following is one of the many possibilities of showing the development of the letter.

OUTLINE

The Prologue: The Word We Have Seen. I John 1:1-4

The Theme of the Letter: God Is Light. I John 1:5—2:29
    The Theme Stated: God Is Light (1:5)
    God Is Light: Tested by a Righteous Walk in Light (1:6—2:6)
    God Is Light: Tested by the Life of Love (2:7-17)
    God Is Light: Tested by True Belief (2:18-29)

The Theme Developed: What It Means to Be Children of God.
    I John 3:1—4:6
    The Theme Restated: What It Means to Be Children of God
    (3:1-2)
    Being Children of God Means Living in God's Purity (3:3-10)
    Being Children of God Means Living in Love (3:11-24)
    Being Children of God Means Distinguishing Truth from Error
    (4:1-6)

The Unifying Summary: God Is Love. I John 4:7-21

The Relation of Love and Faith. I John 5:1-12

The True Knowledge. I John 5:13-21

COMMENTARY

THE PROLOGUE: THE WORD WE HAVE SEEN
I John 1:1-4

Almost everyone who reads his Bible at all is conscious of the fact that the Fourth Gospel begins with a prologue, "In the beginning was the Word . . ." (John 1:1-18). The First Letter of John opens in strikingly similar style, its prologue being proportionate in length to this shorter composition. Moreover, the prologue to the letter is concerned with the same central figure as the opening paragraph of the Gospel: Jesus as the Word of God. But the prologue to the Gospel emphasizes the eternal nature of God's Word, his complete oneness with God himself, and his agency in creation, as background for its stirring insistence that "the Word became flesh and dwelt among us" (John 1:14). The letter, on the other hand, stresses this presence of the Word in the midst of men. But there is here the same grand assertion that characterizes the Gospel, namely, that this very human Word of God is "That which was from the beginning."

We have already noted how eager John is to make his readers realize that Christ is real. Not only in the philosopher's distinction between spirit and matter, but also in the daily round of life men find it hard to believe that such a one as Jesus actually lived. What place has the eternal Christ in our time schedule? John, who was as conscious of living in the world as any of us, came to grips with this question and he was insistent that he knew the answer. He and the others who proclaimed Jesus as the Christ had actually handled him as a fellow man. In his concern to make this experience real he writes of Christ as quite objective, someone who may be looked upon and seen. Perhaps this is the reason he says "That which" instead of "He who." Christ was from an utterly other world than ours, God's world, and yet he lived amongst us as a real man.

But why should One who belonged to God's world become part of ours? Were not the Gnostics right in being disgusted with such a crassly material thought? No, for the purpose is clear. It is so that God's very life should become our life. It is "the life" that "was made manifest," it is "the eternal life" which is not only with God but is revealed to us, and is made our actual possession.

We shall see later just what John thinks of the real nature of this
eternal life, but it is significant that at the very beginning of his
letter he introduces the thought as the reason for Christ's uniting
the world of God with the world of man.

But there is another purpose, also characteristically important
in the eyes of this writer. Christ has brought the spiritual order
into our material world so that those who saw him may know
that "our fellowship is with the Father and with his Son Jesus
Christ." And John is proclaiming this same truth to his readers
"so that you may have fellowship with us." Mystic contempla-
tion of God does not satisfy. A bowing acquaintance with those
who have seen the Lord is not enough. Complete fellowship—
among believers on earth and between earth and heaven—is the
actual goal of the Christian life.

THE THEME OF THE LETTER: GOD IS LIGHT
I John 1:5—2:29

The Theme Stated: God Is Light (1:5)

Fellowship with God and our fellow Christians is not possible
when we live in moral darkness. But we do not need to be in the
dark, because God himself is light. He has made himself known
as the God of a holy love. Nothing about him is kept in the dark;
hence we may walk in the light.

To believe that God is altogether light takes a great deal of
faith. The way is so often dark that he who made the way seems
dark also. The world is so different from God, so estranged from
him, that we feel we cannot see him. Moreover, how is it possible
for the ineffably heavenly light to be seen by worldlings like ourselves? Such fears become all the more tempting in the hours of
men's consciousness of failure. Since mankind has failed in repeated efforts to live in anything approaching a human family, to
speak of our fellowship as being lighted by the divine seems near
to blasphemy. It is out of such considerations that a generation
straining to keep its head up in the wake of wars of world pro-
portions has come to think of God as being at a respectful distance; the transcendence of God has come in for new emphasis.

It is always the glorious message of the Christ that while God
is highly exalted, yet he has shone in upon the hearts of men.
"The kingdom of God is at hand" was Jesus' first message (Mark

1:15). The gospel speaks of a God who is revealed; he has made himself known; he is light, not darkness. In spite of sin and evil we can see him without obstruction, for "in him is no darkness at all."

God Is Light: Tested by a Righteous Walk in Light (1:6—2:6)

John is abrupt in his dealing with the impetuous folly of those who claim fellowship with the God of light and then live a dark life (1:6). The life of fellowship is a life that first of all is cleansed from sin by the given life of Jesus (1:7). Rushing pell-mell into the presence of God's light might even lead a man to deny that he has any darkness within himself. He may claim that he has no sin to be forgiven. But such a man is only self-deceived (1:8), and if he perseveres in his false pride he makes God himself out to be a liar, for God has never taken sin lightly (1:10). It is only willingness to face the blackness in our own lives, however embarrassing this may be, that can lead to the cleansed sense of forgiveness, the humbling experience that must precede all true fellowship (1:9). One cannot heedlessly rush into the presence of even another man, and claim his comradeship. How much less may a man rush uncleansed into fellowship with the pure God! This is not to contradict John's urgent teaching that God is light, nor is it to make God at all withdrawn or unwilling to share his light. But it is to recognize that light and darkness are opposites, and that unless a man is willing to have all that he is exposed to the light, the whole idea of living with God is but playing with life.

The purpose of writing in such a vein, John reminds his readers, is to get them out of the life of sin (2:1). Yet John is ever the realist; he knows that his readers will at some time fall into sin. And so at this point he reminds them that part of God's illuminating work is to present Jesus Christ both as the "advocate" for men who have sinned (as though he were pleading their case at the bar) and also the "expiation" for sins, the one who washes them away (2:1-2). In his idea of the advocate John resembles Paul, who often makes use of legal figures to express man's relation with God. But in the picture of Christ as expiation we have a thought that goes beyond any courtroom scene to the most refreshing figure of cleansing, that of a stream flowing freely. Sometimes the beauty of this thought has been missed when the term for expiation has been translated as though it meant "propitiation." But neither in the writings of Paul nor in those of John is God thought of as a standoff, offended deity who has to be "propitiated" or appeased before he will act favorably. Rather does the course of his love run free in the cleansing of sin. It is this that makes real fellowship possible.

We may never be sure that we "know" God, as the prideful Gnostics of all ages think that they know him easily, unless this cleansing has taken place. And we can test whether it has taken place, says John, only by our willingness to "keep his commandments" (2.3). This is not the laying down of some cold rule of practice, but rather an insistence that the forgiven heart is ready to do the will of him who forgave. To keep God's word is to find God's love perfected within the heart (2:5).

God Is Light: Tested by the Life of Love (2:7-17)

If we have the courage to believe that God is actually light in a world of darkness, then the sincerity of our belief faces another test. We must not only live cleansed lives of personal purity, but also lives of love. John is very clear about this. Love and hate are mortal enemies. To tolerate hatred for someone else, even a little hatred, is to live a dark and gloomy life which really denies that God is light (2:9). Our psychologists are reminding us that resentment held for even a short period upsets the normal functions of the stomach and liver and other organs. The trouble with most men is that they do not quite recognize when they are really hating someone else. They live as though they are blindfolded.

So it is that John calls this distinction between the light of love and the darkness of hate both a new and an old commandment (2:7-8). It is old in the sense that such a difference has always been true in life. It is new in the sense that Christ has come as the true light to make it unmistakably clear. It is easy to look with accustomed eyes at an old scene year after year and not really perceive what is there, and then suddenly, as with new eyes, to see for the first time something that had been there all along. So it is with Christ's revelation of the way of light. We see plainly once for all what we dimly knew was true, that to cherish bitterness is to stumble along in a darkened life, while to open the heart to self-giving love is to come out into the sunlight (2:10-11).

John is so imbued with the importance of this distinction that he repeats himself even more than usual in driving it home. The elaborate parallelism of 2:12-14 is puzzling. John addresses his

audience twice as "children," "fathers," and "young men," and
he twice states augustly that he is penning this important message
to each of them. This sounds as though he is thinking of the Christian Church as made up of three age groups—children, youth,
and elder men. Yet the words used for "children" in the two
rounds are different, and it is more probable that he is in each
case addressing all Christians and representing them to be children of God, youthful in their outlook, and having the responsibility of fathers of families. The tenses used in the two rounds are
different too, and it is quite likely that John intended in this
formal way to make his readers pause and consider how inti-
mately he was addressing them. To all such readers, of every age
in life, he would show the connection between a life that has
"overcome the evil one" and one that loves.

This is more important than we may think. The heart that
hates another, for whatever cause, even if it hates what it feels
is false in the other, exposes itself to false living on its own part.
The surest safeguard against yielding to temptation is to expend
one's energies in love. John proceeds to warn his fellow Christians
not to use love upon the wrong objects (2:15-17). To "love the
world" is to prevent God's love from having leeway. The "world"
always means for this writer the sphere of evil. It is possible to
use the term in other ways. God made the world and it is his;
God loves the world even when it has gone wrong. We are right
in singing, "This is my Father's world." And yet the idea of
"worldliness" as used here is entirely correct also. It is the opposite to goodness, and John, with his absolute contrasts, centers
on such extreme differences. For all who feel the pull of worldly
lusts and ambitions, John insists that this pull does not last long.
When one is young and strong it is hard to believe that "the world
passes away, and the lust of it"; perhaps it is still harder to envision the fact that "he who does the will of God abides for ever."
But this is John's faith in "eternal life," and his conviction that
this eternal life is the life of love.

God Is Light: Tested by True Belief (2:18-29)

We are inclined to feel that beliefs do not matter. Some of
them, indeed, scarcely do. But John goes to the deeps of living
when he tests our appreciation of God as light, not only by purity
of life and by readiness to love, but also by a careful examination of what we believe. And for John all true belief centers in

Christ as the revelation of God. Not to believe this is to be an
"antichrist" (2:22). The idea of an antichrist who would be the
direct opponent of God's Christ was popular in the days of the
Early Church. Usually only one antichrist was thought of. But
John thinks of anyone as antichrist whose *spirit* is opposed to the
belief in Christ as God's revealing light: "many antichrists have
come" (2:18).

In common with most Christians of our early era John held
also that "the end" was close at hand. He says that "it is the last
hour" (2:18). Now if these early Christians meant by this the end
of the world, in the outward sense of the destruction of the universe, they were of course mistaken. But it is quite probable that
they did not mean that at all. John thought of the "world" as the
sphere of evil which is opposed to the love and light of God. It
would be in keeping with that idea if by "the last hour" he meant
that the power of the world over Christ's followers was having its
final fling. If so, this is an urgency which we may repeat in any
age. It is always the "last hour" of evil for the followers of Christ
who strongly believe that God has showed his light in the love of
Christ, that Christ is real and is no dream. John is quite explicit
about this. The "antichrist" is always the one who denies that
Jesus is God's Christ, and he is always a "liar" (2:22). That is to
say, the man of the first century who was too fastidious about his
faith to believe that the eternal God would dwell in worldly human flesh was actually denying God's love and light.

It may be hard for the modern Christian to make the transfer.
But anyone who fears that Christ is unreal, that his life of self-
giving was a pretty ideal but one impossible to follow in our
workaday world, anyone who feels that Jesus' moral require-
ments are too hard or too unrelated to life, is in the same way
denying Christ as the revelation of God. We become antichrists
whenever we live as though Christ were not thinkable.

It is well to note what John says is the outcome for these who
thus deny the reality of Christ. "They went out from us, but they
were not of us" (2:19). John seems never to think it necessary
to *put* anyone out of the Church. For he seems to feel that the
fellowship in Christ is so strong that anyone who does not have
it will not be able to tolerate the atmosphere; he will simply go
out. Where the Church's oneness is such as to make this real, it
is a much finer discipline than any outward punishment or expul-
sion. Thus the fellowship of belief does not tie itself to a particu-

lar form of words that men accept, but to an understanding of God's Christ.

And how does such understanding come? Not through imparted information, but through being "anointed by the Holy One" (2:20, 27). The "Holy One" is the Holy Spirit, and, as John sees it, it is the Spirit's function to give knowledge. To see light under the power of the guidance of the Spirit is to *know* in a sense which can result from no human instruction. It is the Christian answer to the Gnostic—the "knower"—who is proud of his secret, mystic knowledge, an answer which comes to the one who lives simply and humbly the life of righteousness and of love and of loyal belief in the reality of Christ. He intuitively learns the mind of God—knows the Christ.

THE THEME DEVELOPED: WHAT IT MEANS TO BE CHILDREN OF GOD
I John 3:1—4:6

The Theme Restated: What It Means to Be Children of God (3:1-2)

Like a poet trying many possible ways of expressing his thought, or a musician playing variations on his theme, John restates his message. "God is light" definitely implies that God loves. And with what love! We do not have to wait for some future life to know the meaning of that love; we know it now. And we know it in the simplest terms: we are his children. As the little child feels perfectly at home with his parents, so we feel if we recognize God as truly our Father. It does not matter then that we know so little of what shall be in the future; we are content to rest in the assurance that "we shall see him as he is" (3:2).

Being Children of God Means Living in God's Purity (3:3-10)

As we have already seen, John never leaves a principle in the abstract; he brings it down to everyday affairs. And, in line with his tendency to repeat in form as well as in ideas, he shows that being the children of God means something definite in pure living, in love, and in right belief. In the same way we have noted that the author's first statement of his theme, "God is light," is developed by way of right living, and love, and true belief.

But in this second round of his spiral John goes much further than he did the first time. His love of absolute contrasts carries him to great extremes. He not only makes it clear that being a child of God makes one pure, but he insists that since Christ has no sin and has come to take away sins (3:5), therefore no one can abide in him and at the same time commit sin (3:6). To have God's nature in oneself is to be "born of God," and therefore the follower of God finds it as impossible to sin as it is for God (3:9). If one does sin he has been born, not of God, but of the Devil (3:8). The contrast between the children of the Devil and the children of God is clear to anyone who will look upon this difference (3:10).

Such extreme statements have caused no little dissension in the Church. They have led some to rule out the First Letter of John as impossible. They have caused others to become "perfectionist" in their ideas of the Christian life and to imagine themselves incapable of sin. But John would be contradicting himself if he were stating perfectionism. He has already taught clearly that we all have sin to confess (1:8-9), and he later contemplates our praying for those who commit sin, but the kind that is not "mortal," that is, not a deliberate and deadly setting of themselves against God (5:16-17).

This should give us the clue to John's thought. It is not going deep enough to say, as some have done, that John is contrasting living in a state of sin with committing an occasional act. That is true as far as it goes. But John's habit of thought, as we have seen, is the complete contrast. He is saying that there are two kinds of children born into the world—children of the Devil and children of God. The children of the Devil find sin natural, for the Devil is a constant sinner. The children of God find sin totally out of keeping with their nature, since God cannot sin. Such a contrast, extreme as it is, is worth making. It is a most powerful call to take life seriously. The Gnostics were always talking about birth from divine seed. They thought of this, not as entailing responsibility, but as putting them on the lofty scale of privilege. John says that to be born of God's seed brings clear obligation to pure living, since God is pure.

Such absolute contrasts are not out of keeping with the rest of Scripture. In the Gospel of John the author develops the same extreme difference between the followers of Christ and his enemies, representing them as born of two different lines. "You are of your father the devil," Jesus bluntly tells his opponents (John 8:44). In the Sermon on the Mount, Jesus is pictured as stating just such a sharp contrast: "A sound tree cannot bear evil fruit" (Matt. 7:18). Even Paul, who generally avoids language which might be interpreted as teaching perfectionism, says, in discussing our going to the Cross with Christ, "For he who has died is freed from sin" (Rom. 6:7). Moreover, the complete destruction of "the works of the devil" which John envisions here (3:8), as indeed the destruction of the Devil himself, is a common New Testament theme. When the disciples returned from a successful mission of healing, Christ is recorded as having said, "I saw Satan fall like lightning from heaven" (Luke 10:18). At the visit of the Greeks he could exclaim, "Now shall the ruler of this world be cast out" (John 12:31). And Paul represents God as triumphing over the principalities and powers in Christ (Col. 2:15). The Book of Revelation is full of repeated assurances of the impending end of the Devil himself, even as his kingdom has already ceased to rule in the hearts of Christ's followers. So it is in line with Christian truth for John to call here for faith in the God who is able to keep those who have been born of his seed. This is a dynamic both for confidence and for high living. It is the letter's statement of the same high doctrine of life which we find in the Gospel's teaching of the new birth (John 3:3-7). It is cause for constant gratitude, never for pride.

Being Children of God Means Living in Love (3:11-24)

Just how closely John interweaves his thought is especially demonstrated in this passage. To be children of God means not only to live rightly but to love truly. The example of the opposite way of life is Cain. This son of Adam failed to love his brother Abel. But why did he not love? According to John, "Because his own deeds were evil and his brother's righteous" (3:12). Lack of love is the result of bad living. Conversely, bad living produces the jealousy that grows into hate and murder. It is only a worldly disposition that hates (3:13). Not to love is to remain in death; to love is to gain the assurance that we have already passed from death to life (3:14).

But again John cannot leave such high principles in the air. He must bring them down to the everyday. The test of real love was, in the case of Christ, his laying down his life for us; so also the test of the reality of our own love for our brother is our readiness to go the limit and give our life for him (3:16). Yet giving life does not mean simply some grand and heroic sacrifice.

It means the open heart and the ready hand whenever we see our brother in need (3:17). This is the way to love in what John calls the "truth" instead of mere repetition of the sentimental phrases of affection (3:18).

For hearts that have learned to love like this our author has a remarkable testimony. It is nothing less than this: if our own hearts do not condemn us—that is, for any lack of readiness in love—God will never prove sharper in judgment than our own hearts but will show himself even more gracious than our hearts can be to ourselves, so that we may have full confidence before him (3:21).

Being Children of God Means Distinguishing Truth from Error (4:1-6)

Again John turns to right belief as parallel to right living and right loving. He has already suggested anew the relation of love and belief by connecting belief in Christ with love of one another (3:23). Moreover, he has prefaced this passage with the key word "Spirit" to indicate the one who confirms our assurance of love (3:24).

This word suggests to John the negative evil spirit as the opposite of God's Holy Spirit, even as John always balances the positive and the negative. So he can say, "Beloved, do not believe every spirit" (4:1). This throws the responsibility for decision on the individual believer. Some of the spirits of the world are very persuasive. But again John makes the test practical, and he directs it at the great evil of his day. Not to believe that Jesus has come in the flesh is the falsehood of an evil spirit (4:2-3). As before, the author associates such a spirit with what he calls "antichrist" (4:3; see 2:18). He is certain that his readers can distinguish false spirits in the world from God's true Spirit by this simple test of belief in the real flesh-and-blood life of the Son of God (4:2).

Such reasoning may seem far removed from our time. But is it? The simple assurance of John (4:5-6) sounds quite dogmatic. Taken out of its context it would be just that. But in its relation to the assuring presence of the Spirit of God, we, too, may experience the confidence that certain thoughts are right and others are error, that certain people are true believers and others are not. To assume such positive positions on our own initiative would be arrogant. To learn to see them with the swift insight of those who are led by the Spirit is victorious living.

THE UNIFYING SUMMARY: GOD IS LOVE
I John 4:7-21

Life always needs some power to bind its loose ends together. John, by his statement, "God is light" (1:5), has already made crystal-clear his thought of God as self-revealed. Now he summarizes all our relation to him by this great new assertion, "God is love" (4:8, 16). Note that he does not content himself with saying, "God is loving"—that is, that God has a loving disposition—but that his very essence is love. All love inheres in him. We would never know how to love anyone if this were not so. Our human nature could never create love; its source is in God, "for love is of God" (4:7). Moreover, if God were simply light and not also love, that light would be unbearable. John flatly denies that we are able to love God; it is God who loves us (4:10). Verse 19, "We love, because he first loved us," goes even further, with the statement that we are enabled to love other people because of what God's love has done in us.

Our love to one another is the return we make on his love to us. We perceive God as light when we love one another (4:12). Our love to one another must be self-giving just as God's love to us is the gift of his Son to cleanse us from our sins (4:10).

Without God's love in our lives we would be forced to cower in fear. The terrible dreads that lay many men and women low are the result of lack of love. But love, so far as it is perfected in our lives, completely casts out fear (4:18). There is more said about fear today than ever before. Our psychologists study the causes and cures of fear. We are taught to trace our personal terrors back to some earlier experience. We learn about fear complexes. And all this has its place. Some fears can be cured scientifically. Learn that the cause of them was foolish and has disappeared, and the fear will go too. But the deeper dreads of life can be cured by love alone. The fear of other people can be overcome only as we learn to give ourselves willingly to them. The fright that some people experience at the thought of God can be relieved only when they come to trust that God himself is love. It is for this reason that John can say that even our dread of God's judgment disappears when we know love (4:17). Hence the grand assertion that belief in God's love as it is seen in the gift of his Son enables us quietly to abide in him (4:13).

THE RELATION OF LOVE AND FAITH
I John 5:1-12

John's thought is never far removed from the interplay of love and righteous living and true belief. Here he insists again upon the relation between faith and love. To believe that Jesus is the Christ is to be a child of God, so that faith brings one into loving relationship to God. Such love for God makes love for the other children of God an assured fact (5:1). It is this confidence that leads our author to make use of one of his most characteristic thoughts—the identification of love and keeping the command-ments of God (5:2-3). If we think of a commandment in the sense of some stern requirement laid on us, this would be distaste-ful. But when we realize that we are children of God's love, then his every will is our delight to perform, just as the lover says to his beloved, "Your least command is my joy."

For the child of God the commandments of God, including the command to love, are not a burden, says John, because it is the way to overcome the world (5:4). As a matter of fact, it is our faith in this love that does overcome the world. John has written a great deal about "believing"; this is the only place in his writings where he uses the *noun* "faith." To him faith is victory—not a triumph over what the proud Gnostic would call the world of evil matter, but over what the Christian thinks of as the world of moral wrong. It is love that begets the faith to win the victory over wrong, and this is the only victory that is important.

At this point John introduces what may seem to us to be a strange line of argument. He talks about our belief in the three witnesses, the Spirit, the water, and the blood (5:8). Indeed, in the entire paragraph (5:6-12) he has these three primarily in mind. Here again is his answer to the "Seemists" of his day, to those who liked to scoff at Jesus because he only seemed to be a real man. There were some who even went so far as to suggest that Jesus did not have the Spirit of God within him during all of his life. They said that the Spirit came upon him only at the time of his baptism—this is what John refers to when he says "the water"—and left him again at his crucifixion—this is what is referred to by "the blood." But John insists that Christ had the Spirit all along and that this Spirit testifies at every point of his life—baptism and condemnation and all. Such a belief cannot be proved in any worldly sense; it must be known spiritually as a "testimony" which a Christian has come to have within himself (5:10). And the issue of this testimony is "eternal life," not a vague promise of something to be by and by, but a present possession: "He who has the Son has life" (5:12). In fact, life that is ours now always has this quality of the eternal because it is inherent in God's Son (5:11). This is the uniquely Christian view. Paul also taught it as a present experience (Rom. 6:11, 23). And the Gospel of John echoes the same thought (John 5:25; 11:26). No more wonderful claim could be made for the Christian life!

THE TRUE KNOWLEDGE
I John 5:13-21

It would be almost unthinkable that John should close this trenchant letter without giving expression to the glories of true Christian knowledge. He has been dealing all along with the "knowers," those who pridefully preen themselves on their innate ability to fathom the meaning of life. He has insisted that this kind of knowledge is deadly. It is the kind that Paul called the knowledge that "puffs up" (I Cor. 8:1). John had put in place of such boastful arrogance his insistence that it is love and belief in Christ and right living that are important.

But after all, knowledge has its place. It is as though John had been saving his finest shot for the last. He will show the "knowers" what the Christian really knows. Over and over in these few verses John rings out the message of assurance: "We know . . . we know . . . we know." We know that we have eternal life, that he hears us when we ask of him, and that our requests of him are answered (5:13, 15). This is the faith of a child who knows his parent and who trusts that parent's love. We know that to be born of God is the opposite of being born in sin (5:18). We know that we belong to God and that the moral worldling belongs to "the evil one" (5:19). We know that it is God's Son who gives us the understanding of life so that we may know him who is true; that is, that we may know God (5:20). This is the highest possible attainment in life, provided it is knowledge of the kind of God who has revealed himself in the Son of his love (5:20). Any other kind of god is an idol, and to keep oneself from idols is the converse side of belonging to the true God (5:21).

JOHN

The Nature of the Letter

This, the briefest of all the compositions in our New Testament, is an affectionate note from the "elder" to the "elect lady and her children" (vs. 1). Such a form of address seems most naturally to suggest correspondence between individuals. And since the Third Letter begins in the same way, as a note addressed from the "elder" to an individual who is named—Gaius—this is quite possible. Moreover, the text may be translated "the lady Electa." If this were the correct translation we would have in each of these the name of the person addressed in these short letters. But, in accordance with the habits of letter writers of old, more probably this is a pleasing way of addressing a particular church. A "chosen" or "elect" church sends greetings to a sister church (vs. 13), as a church group does in I Peter 5:13.

The mood of this brief message is authoritative. The "elder" means to use all his influence with the church to which he is writing, and to utter his counsel with no uncertain voice. That he is the same writer as the author of the longer First John is seen by the occurrence of the same words and ideas, such as the fact that love is a commandment that is not new (vs. 5), that truth is a way to walk in or to follow (vs. 4), that antichrist is a spirit of evil that gets into men (vs. 7). Again we meet the strong assertion that Jesus Christ is the Son of God (vs. 3), and that he has really come in the flesh in spite of the "deceivers"— the "Seemists" again, as in First John—who go abroad teaching that he only appeared to be real (vs. 7).

The Controversy

The controversial tone of this little letter becomes what many would call "narrow." The elder rails against anyone who "goes ahead" and who does not "abide in the doctrine of Christ" (vs.

28

9), and he advises the church to refuse hospitality to any who
do not hold to the reality of Christ, and even not to greet them
(vs. 10). He does not want true followers of the Christ to "share"
in such work, or, more literally, to "fellowship" in it.

We may have to bury some of our prejudices in order to realize how important this struggle was in the Early Church. The
question of the person of Christ was hotly debated for a long
time. If the leaders of the Church had not at times seemed dogmatic in their stand for the genuineness of Jesus' life and ministry, they would have permitted their new and untried disciples
to drift away from him. Dogmatism that may sound cold and
self-opinionated in an environment where there is highly developed training and understanding, may be but a father's caution
to young children. This is the attitude of the elder. Verse 9 is
not to be taken as a diatribe against all kinds of progress, but as
a warning against that sort of restless instability which never
"stays put" in its faith.

We may clearly recognize the same tendencies in the life of
today. Just as there is a cult of conservatism for conservatism's
sake, which is provokingly standpat in all its thought and action,
so also there is a cult of progressivism for progressivism's sake
which is wild and foolish. To us, as well as to first-century Christians, especially if we are still inclined to be babes in Christ, there
may come the needed injunction, "Look to yourselves, that you
may not lose what you have worked for" (vs. 8)—a saying which
finds an interesting parallel in John's letter to the church at
Philadelphia, "Hold fast what you have, so that no one may seize
your crown" (Rev. 3:11).

That the author is reluctant to write to the church about matters so personal, and is doing so only to meet an emergency
before he can get to them in person, is evidenced by the homely
expression of frustration in the use of "paper and ink," a frustration which all of us, in this age of poor letter writing, may share.
In any age it is true that to talk "face to face" is to make "joy . . .
complete" (vs. 12).

THE THIRD LETTER OF

JOHN

The Problem of the Letter

The similarity of this letter to the one preceding is evident. Again it is the "elder" writing, and he is conscious once more of the need of exercising his "authority" (vs. 9). The words "love" and "truth" stand out (vss. 1, 3, 4, 6, 8, 12) as in the other letters by this author, and truth is once more not so much a creed to be believed as a way in which to walk (vs. 4). The Christian life must be really good to be of God (vs. 11).

But the problem of this letter may be said to be that of Second John in reverse. Whereas in the former letter there were heretics making the rounds of the churches and disturbing the faith of many, in this case it is the missionaries of the Church who are on circuit (vss. 5-8). And while, in the earlier case, the elder found it necessary to urge the churches not to receive the heretics lest they contaminate the fellowship by their false teaching, here he pleads for hospitality. The bitter struggle for supremacy in the Early Church and the selfish pride of one man, Diotrephes, is reflected in the extreme to which such a man will go. He not only will not practice hospitality toward the itinerant missionaries himself, but he tries to prohibit anyone else in the Church from entertaining them, even putting such hospitable Christians out of the Church when they do (vs. 10).

The letter is addressed to "the beloved Gaius" (vs. 1), who seems to be standing almost alone in his cordial reception of the traveling preachers and in helping them on their way. Apparently the writer has received repeated testimony to the kindliness of Gaius (vss. 3, 6), not only from the Church itself but also from those who have been welcomed by him when they were strangers (vs. 5). The reference to what the elder has already written the Church (vs. 9) may refer to Second John or to some other bit of correspondence he has had with these Christians.

Development of the Problem

Our practical minds may raise the question, how can one tell when he should welcome unknown teachers of the Word, as this Third Letter of John warmly recommends, and when he should shy from all fellowship with newcomers who would teach in the Church, as the Second Letter warns. John's answer would be clear: Whoever preaches Jesus as the Son of God really come in the flesh, sharing all our woes and manner of life, cleansing us from our sins, revealing the nature of God as love—whoever speaks in this vein is to be welcomed and aided. But whoever—in the name of a deeper understanding, a "Gnosticism" that is proud in its so-called "knowledge"—goes on to leave Christ out as unreal or unnecessary, that man is to be rejected at once. Such distinctions may seem hard to make, especially where friends have become involved in new and strange teachings. But there should be a sharpness to Christian judgment if the Church is to be kept pure. And once again, this purity is nothing formal, but has to do with everyday living which always needs the grace and power of Christ.

That the writer recognizes the difficulty of discussing such personal involvements with "pen and ink," as he did in the Second Letter, is again clear (vs. 13), and again there is expressed the longing to see friends "face to face" and reach the deepest understanding (vs. 14). And so, greetings to friends are extended with the charge that they be given to "every one of them" (vs. 15). Such is the tenderness and grace of real Christian fellowship.

JUDE

INTRODUCTION

The Problem

Many a Christian leader, eager to advance some deep line of thought or some new activity, has found instead that he has to go back and ground his followers on the foundations or protect them from a surprise danger. The author of the Letter to the Hebrews had to wrestle with the problem of going on from "the elementary doctrines" to what he called "maturity" (Heb. 6:1-3). So also with the author of this little Letter of Jude. He had anxiously sought opportunity to write to his Christian friends about "our common salvation," but was reduced to the necessity of realizing that his readers were facing "ungodly persons" who had "secretly gained" entrance into the Church and whose low and crafty ways were understood but little. To guard their would-be victims against rapid inroads, he feels that mere defense is not enough; they must "contend for the faith" (vss. 3-4). "Faith" is thus understood to be not primarily a trust in God's righteousness, as it was for Paul (Rom. 3:21-31), nor yet sublime confidence in God's providence, as Jesus had taught his disciples (Matt. 6:25-34), nor even a present-day grasp on the hope of the future, as another great New Testament writer had described it (Heb. 11:1). But with the Letter of Jude we have reached a time in the Church when "faith" has become a tradition, a deposit of what the early Christians believed, a creed—potent for living but still a definite body of truth that could be spelled out and fought for. It was something that had been "once for all delivered to the saints" (vs. 3).

Yet this letter is not simply a call to do battle for a position. Nowhere in the New Testament do you find writers who are concerned about intellectual heresy for its own sake. It is clear here, as elsewhere, that what disturbs the writer is the relation of false belief to false living. The intruders whom he opposes are "ungodly persons" who not only "deny . . . Jesus Christ" but who "pervert the grace of our God into licentiousness" (vs. 4). Perhaps it is not easy for us to see the importance of this connection. If one's belief is simply peculiar, if he is "off," as we say, at some point of understanding, but without any effect on his good life, then he is not particularly dangerous to the Church. He is apt to get straightened out in time, for his good will is bound to enable him to learn from others. But if one is vicious, if he twists the meaning of his faith in such a way as to make his error in belief the feeder of his craving for immoral conduct, then he can upset the Church very quickly. He perverts the very grace of God, as Jude says.

So it was that Jude felt it to be immediately necessary to warn his people against such hypocrites. He displays a vividness of style and a passionate concern that are worthy of the best. The imagery under which he attacks the false leaders in the Church is gruesome at times, but it has an originality and fire and finality about it that make it ever memorable. The author of Second Peter later found it so to his liking that when he, too, felt called upon to warn the Church against evil within it he borrowed many of the figures of this forthright and compelling writer (see II Peter 2).

The Author and the Destination

Who was the man who thus made bold to leap into the midst of a dangerous situation? And who were the people to whom he wrote? The letter itself gives us no clear answer, and tradition concerning it is late and hardly very reliable. The author calls himself "a servant [or slave] of Jesus Christ," and also "brother of James" (vs. 1). The first of these titles could apply to any devoted Christian leader. Paul often thinks of himself as Christ's slave (Rom. 1:1; Phil. 1:1; Titus 1:1). Under the second title the writer is apparently seeking to identify himself with the family of the James who was the head of the Jerusalem church, and thus indirectly with Jesus himself, since this James was a brother of the Lord. Thus his authority would be enhanced and the people would be the more apt to heed what he wrote. He writes simply to "those who are called" (vs. 1), again a general designation that does not suggest any particular destination for the letter.

COMMENTARY

Greeting (Vss. 1-2)

To those who are God's select ones Jude writes, extending as a servant of Christ his prayers for "mercy, peace, and love" not only to rest upon them but to be increased. The mood of the verb here is one seldom used in the New Testament. It denotes ardent desire. The writer is urgent that the Christian graces of his readers be "multiplied," as though he feels that they will need a good deal more of God's mercy and of inner peace and of love in their hearts if they are to withstand the insidious evil that is in their midst.

Reason for Writing (Vss. 3-4)

These verses make clear the writer's intent to develop a real treatise on salvation, but his decision is to put this aside for the meeting of the immediate danger. That those who teach wrongly and practice viciousness are actually the same sort of docetic Gnostics whom we met with in the First Letter of John is likely from the statement that they "deny our only Master." That is, they probably deny that Jesus, God's pure Son, could have come in such evil form as human flesh. Thus meekly pretending that they recognize that all flesh is evil, they cover up their own evil ways which are contrary to the goodness of human life as God made it.

Gross Sin Is Always Punished (Vss. 5-7)

Before describing in detail what the wicked men in the Church are like, Jude pauses to assure his readers that all evil is eventually punished. He draws three illustrations. Some of those whom God himself delivered out of Egypt he afterward destroyed because they did not really believe in him (vs. 5); the angels who fell from their state of holy submission are now in chains (vs. 6); and communities like Sodom and Gomorrah, which "indulged in unnatural lust," have been brought down to the very pit of hell (vs. 7). The first and last of these are well known. The story of the fallen angels gets its start from Genesis 6:1-4, but is developed in the apocryphal Book of Enoch on which Jude draws freely. The Jewish Christians of the first century were doubtless familiar with tales of the horror suffered by the angels who were impious enough to rebel against God, so that to compare some of their own leaders to these terrible beings would have immediately impressed them.

False Leaders in the Church Are Basically Irreverent (Vss. 8-10)

Just as the fallen angels began with the sin of impiety, so also have these leaders in the Church dared to fly in the face of God. Their lives are characterized by the rejection of authority and the spirit of reviling. To emphasize this by way of contrast, Jude goes to another apocryphal book, called The Assumption of Moses, which seems to have been greatly relished by the religious people of his day. Here he found the story of the archangel Michael, a tale developed from the scriptural account of God's burial of Moses in the mountain (Deut. 34). The Devil is supposed to have desired to possess Moses' body. Michael, leading the hosts of God, disputed his right, but Michael was polite even in dealing with the Devil; "he did not presume to pronounce a reviling judgment," but left him to God. After all, the Devil was a fallen angel, and Michael did not act impiously toward him. Yet the false leaders of Jude's day dare to act impiously against God himself! They are "as irrational animals."

Passionate Denunciation of the Immoral Leaders (Vss. 11-13)

The writer is genuinely and righteously enraged at the evil he has beheld. He denounces the false leaders, comparing them to three weak villains of old: Cain, Balaam, and Korah (vs. 11). Cain's wickedness culminated in the murder of his brother (Gen. 4:1-8). Cain was used as typical of all evil in many of the Jewish writings of the general period of Jude. Balaam's error—associated by Jude with covetousness—kept him from getting the blessing of Israel's God, whom he knew though he was a Moabite (Num., chs. 22-24; 31:16). Korah was the rebel who nearly overthrew Moses' leadership at a critical time in Israel's history (Num. 16:1-34). With these three as background the writer uses some of the most picturesque imagery in the entire New Testament to condemn the leadership of his day. They make a carousal out of the love feast, which was one of the most sacred gatherings of early Christians. Under such figures as hidden "reefs" (margin for "blemishes"), "waterless clouds," "fruitless trees," "wild waves," and "wandering stars," Jude forever makes their reputation notorious (vss. 12-13).

Such Characters Have Long Been Predicted (Vss. 14-19)

The writer does not want his people to feel that they have been especially ill-used because such men have arisen in their day. They were not unexpected. Again he quotes from the Book of Enoch to show that such men were anticipated (vss. 14-16), and also from "the predictions of the apostles" (vs. 17). These last would be the common apostolic teaching that "scoffers" would arise as times grew worse toward the end. "In the last time" (vs. 18) does not necessarily refer to the end of the world in the sense of the destruction of the universe, but to the termination of this world order, as the early Christians generally thought of it. The important thing to note in these verses is that the wicked leaders are described as men of selfish passion and as sectarian in their spirit (vss. 18-19). In earlier days in America the Church tended to glorify the setting up of new denominations as the proof of independent faith. Today we are coming more and more to realize, as Jude seems to have done, that the easy forming of new branches of the Church is apt to grow from a spirit of self-centeredness, from the divisive purpose of those who have an ax to grind.

Positive Activity for a Holy Faith (Vss. 20-23)

Any struggle against evil, however justified, tends to be negative. It is apt to produce people who know what they are *against* but who are not *for* very much. So Jude recommends specific positive actions that men of faith must follow if they are rightly to guard themselves against evil. Faith, prayer, and love are his chief insistences, combined with a humble waiting for the Lord's mercy (vss. 20-21). It is interesting to note that Jude feels that these graces will enable his readers to be at once cautious and kindly, convincing some of those who are rather on the fence and snatching from the burning those who are on the road to destruction (vss. 22-23). Such virtues, well developed, can do more to rescue men from the snares of evil than all the bitter force one may employ.

Benediction (Vss. 24-25)

It is significant that the little letter of Jude closes with one of the most beautiful benedictions in the New Testament. It is as though, with the storm of rage against the evil leaders spent, and with prayer and faith and love built into the Church, the author could now invoke the tenderest of God's care upon his readers. It is an appropriate benediction, for it calls on the One who is able to keep the Church from falling—that is, from falling into the very snares the writer has depicted. It is a hopeful benediction, for it anticipates God's ability to keep the Church without blemish and to do so all through to the time when believers come into the very presence of his glory. It is a positive benediction, because it stresses the note of joy in Christian living. It is a loyal benediction, because it owns Jesus Christ as Lord. And it is an authoritative benediction because it rests its case on the dominion of God in all time to come. Such a blessing will keep evil leaders from gaining spurious authority in any church and will do the utmost to guard the spirits of the faithful.

THE

REVELATION TO JOHN

———

INTRODUCTION

Hard as it seems to believe, the name "Revelation" means exactly what it says. It is intended to be not a hiding of truth, as people often think, but an unfolding. The word "revelation" is derived from the Latin. The corresponding word in the Greek gives us our English word "apocalypse." Literally this denotes the "lifting of the veil," so that it means the same thing as "revelation"—bringing to the light that which is hidden.

But the term "apocalypse" has come to describe not simply the Book of Revelation, but a type of literature with a definite kind of theology, composed mostly by Jews and Jewish Christians at intervals from the days of the Babylonian Exile onwards. Traces of it are to be found in our Old Testament prophets and in some of the later Psalms, but for the most part it is a distinct kind of writing with its own line of thought and its own forms of construction, as definitely marked as the sonnet and the epic style in poetry or the essay and the novel in prose.

Purpose and Message of Apocalyptic

Apocalyptic literature has almost always been composed in times of trial and crisis. It is generally the message of some responsible leader to followers who have been caught in the sudden debacle of misfortune or the suffering of persecution for their faith. It is intended as a kind of private comfort to that faith. For this very reason it has made use of forms of expression and developed doctrines of life that sound somewhat extreme or even peculiar in more ordinary times.

Apocalypse and Prophecy

The relation between the apocalyptic and the prophetic types of literature is close. Both prophet and apocalyptist believe

strongly in one God. Both look upon themselves not only as servants of that God but also as especially inspired by him with a message. Both deal with judgment and hope, with sin and deliverance.
Both anticipate the triumph of God over evil and the rule of God
in the world and the affairs of men.

But the stage of operation and the view of history differ con-
siderably between the two. The prophet is pre-eminently the man
of the Covenant—God's ancient Covenant with Israel—and he
thinks in terms of God's acting within that Covenant. At times,
indeed, he goes beyond God's relations with Israel to speak mes-
sages to or concerning other nations. The groups of oracles
against foreign peoples that characterize portions of our "Major
Prophets" are evidence of this (Isa. 13-23; Jer. 46-51; Ezek. 25-
32). Amos, perhaps the earliest of the writing prophets, pictures
the God of Israel as the judge of all the nations (Amos 1-2).
Habakkuk anticipates God's action against the invading Chal-
deans; Nahum sings of God's wrath against Nineveh. But these
nations are "others"; they are outside the Covenant. Occasionally
a prophet interpreted God's control of the universe as embracing
his relation with other nations as well as with Israel, as when
Amos spoke of God's bringing up "the Philistines from Caphtor
and the Syrians from Kir" in the same breath in which he recalled
the deliverance of Israel from Egypt (Amos 9:7), or as when the
writer of the remarkable passage in Isaiah 19:23-25 thought of
Egypt and Assyria as worshiping with God's people. But more
often the prophets anticipated that if any foreign nation were to
share in the Covenant of God with Israel, it would have to come
up to Jerusalem to the house of God to worship, for from the
Holy City came the blessing. It was in this spirit that Solomon
prayed for the foreigner at the dedication of the Temple (I Kings
8:41-43). It was with this strong emphasis on Israel's Covenant
with God that both Micah and Isaiah sang concerning the day
when the nations should beat their swords into plowshares and
their spears into pruning hooks and should "flow" to Jerusalem
(Isa. 2:2-4; Micah 4:1-5). In the days of the great Prophet of
the Exile we get from the voice of prophecy itself a consistent
view of the universal care of God, universal because Israel has
been appointed God's "Servant" to make God known to all peoples. This theme is developed in Isaiah, chapters 42-53, and is expressed with especially universal emphasis in 49:6.

It was this last view, in the Book of Isaiah, that became typical in the apocalyptical literature. Here all mankind was the field of God's care and activity. Sometimes indeed the figures of Jew and Gentile are used to symbolize those in the Kingdom of God and those in the kingdom of Satan, but these were largely the employment of old and well-known manners of speech. If the apocalyptic writer thought in Covenant terms at all it was mainly of God's Covenant with "Adam," the whole human race.

The Two Worlds

This means that whatever ills flesh is heir to, all the suffering and trouble that can come upon man are the province of the apocalyptist. But in his treatment he is always religious, deeply devout. He is concerned with the connection between trouble and sin, most often the sin of those who cause other men to suffer, and with the crimes committed by agents of the kingdom of Satan against those who belong to the Kingdom of God. For the apocalyptist is ever conscious of two worlds, two kingdoms set against each other. He does not anticipate any slow evolution of the bad into the good; he sees transformation only on the other side of tragedy. He believes always in crisis, in the end of the kind of age he knows. He carries the prophet's teaching of the "Day of the Lord" to its natural conclusion. It becomes a day of the winding up of the powers of darkness and the liberation of the powers of light. Redemption is wrought, not by the gradual sanctifying of those who trust in the Lord, but by their triumph under him in the desperate spiritual conflict that goes on in this world. Hence the apocalyptist is a dualist—that is, one who thinks of two opposing forces—but never the kind that sees two coequal powers at eternal loggerheads with each other. He sees good and evil always personalized as God and Satan, or as Christ and the Devil, but God and God's Christ are always in control of the outcome. The struggle is always moral. Though all kinds of figures of human warfare may be used, it is the fight that goes on in the soul of man, the struggle for the determination of human destiny, that concerns the apocalyptist.

Thus the outcome is foreordained. The apocalyptist recognizes no tentative developments. There is no possibility of several different endings to the story, nor even of two. True, this life may not resolve the struggle, and therefore the apocalyptist looks beyond. It is heaven, not earth, that is his ultimate point of view; or if earth, then the "new earth" of the Book of Revelation. For the prophet, as a rule, *this* life was the good life. He looked for the redemption of his people within time; he expected God to come unto his own in this world. To live with God in the here and now was the great hope. But for the apocalyptist, time is hardly of the essence of reality. Indeed, time is often used as a symbol of the timeless. The life beyond is the great and glorious life to be anticipated by all who suffer and struggle. While the prophet had little or nothing to say about the resurrection life, to the apocalyptist the resurrected life was the grand and glorious anticipation. An apocalypse is really a prophecy staged in eternity.

God as Near and God as Far Away

Prophet and apocalyptist stressed also opposite poles of the relationship between God and man. For the prophet, since "man" was largely Israel and this life the good life, God's nearness was very real. The immanence of God, his closeness to men, was felt so strongly that prophetic writers could picture God sitting in Abraham's tent door and talking with him or meeting with Moses face to face or speaking to an Amos or an Isaiah. The prophet, however harassed by the sins of his people or the dangers of the hour, always lived with the comforting assurance that God was near.

But for the apocalyptist, who thought of this world age as hopeless, who dwelt in dreams of a new age when all mankind would be the children of God, and who often postponed any expectancy of such an age to a world of resurrection beyond the portals of death—for a man with such lofty and envisioned hope God was "high and lifted up," transcendent above the earth that he had made. Not that these contrasts are absolute. The greatest of the prophets could think of God as transcendent, elevated over men and the earth, as the phrase just quoted from Isaiah's call (Isa. 6:1-8) clearly shows. The apocalyptist, too, could at times envision God or the Son of God as drawing near to strengthen and reassure, as when the seer on the Isle of Patmos beheld the "one like a son of man" in the midst of his lampstand churches and experienced the gracious ministry of his strengthening hand (Rev. 1:12-20). But the distinction in emphasis is clear.

It is almost inevitable that such contrasts in emphasis should arise at different periods in the lives of devout men. And while it may not, at first thought, seem much of a comfort to believe in a God so far above that men can know only the outskirts of his ways, yet the human heart stands in need of both the transcendent and the immanent in understanding the divine nature. If the prophet has leaned heavily on the abiding presence of his God in fellowship with him, and if the apocalyptist has gazed in awe at the almost inaccessible holiness of God, we may thank them both for their contributions to our faith and gladly believe that both were inspired.

Yet even the devout apocalyptist could not live entirely on the hope that God would some day be revealed in all his glory. The apocalyptist was human and he must have something substantial for his present-day faith. And so there grew up in the writers of apocalyptic literature the habit of regarding angels (sometimes individual divine messengers to men, but more often a whole host of residents of the courts of God) as the go-betweens in the relations of heaven and earth. The angels became more and more the revealers and interpreters of dreams, the explainers of the future and, perhaps best of all, the encouragement for the present as indicating that the face of God was not entirely withdrawn. For the Jewish apocalyptist the angel was the all-important figure in keeping a sense of contact with God, and for the Christian writer of similar times and circumstances such contact might be expressed in the angel of God's presence or in the vision of the Christ, seated at the right hand of God's power but coming again to be with his Church.

Apocalyptic Style

But apocalyptic literature had not only its special theological points of stress, it developed also its peculiar methods of expression. Because it was usually composed in times of persecution when it was not safe to pass even a message of cheer and hope to like-minded sufferers, the apocalypse often became a cryptogram. It was composed in figures of speech that were known and used among the faithful but totally meaningless to those outside the fold. To decipher such cryptographic writing in the present day is not too difficult, partly because so many apocalypses were written with many of the same figures in each, and partly because in some of these there are hints at interpretation, as when the angel in Fourth Esdras explains certain of the signs, or when at the end of the thirteenth chapter of the Book of Revelation an explanation of the number of the beast, 666, is given.

The Meaning of Cycle

Basic to all apocalyptic writing is the *cycle*. It is the understanding of the apocalyptist that history moves in regularly recurring waves of events and meanings. A cycle is one of a number of intervals or spaces of time in which there is completed some round of happenings that is similar to other successive rounds. We are familiar with the idea in general. We speak of business cycles of prosperity and depression, of the cycle of the seasons, and even of psychological cycles of hope and despair. But very often we take such ideas with a grain of salt or use them only in a highly figurative sense. The apocalyptist takes the cycle quite seriously. He believes that each life and each age goes through its succession of experiences and comes to its own judgment. He sees a certain determinism in the way in which history moves. He is not, however, simply making use of a variety of the "wheel of fate" concept, for he believes that God stands behind all cycles, and that he can and often does intervene to alter their course and issue. Indeed, his cycles may be said to be a grand spiral, mounting ever upward toward the fulfillment of God's eternal purpose.

Important Apocalyptic Figures

Within the cycle many kinds of figures occur, some of them attractive, some bizarre, for life itself has both its glory and its terror. The various kinds of figures are well marked and have a fairly fixed significance in apocalyptic writing.

There are *numbers*. Only a few are used: 3, 3½, 4, 5, 6, 7, 10, 12, and their multiples and squares and cubes. The number 3 always stands for the spirit world; it may be the world of good, as in the case of the last three seals in the Book of Revelation, or it may be the spirit world of evil, as in the case of the last three trumpets in the same book. The number 4, by contrast, is always the earth number, even as we today speak of the "four corners of the earth." Adding the number of the spirit world, 3, and the earth number, 4, you get the complete or perfect number, 7. One half of 7, or 3½, is, logically enough, the incomplete number, the number of something that is cut off, limited. This often appears in apocalypses as 3½ years of persecution or as 42 months or as 1260 days, all of which are approximately the same length of time and suggest the same idea. The number 6, falling just short of the completeness of 7, is the human number, for the apocalyptist always stresses the incompleteness of man. The number 12 suggests God's redeemed company, whether Israel of old or the Church of the Christian era. This is made appropriate, of course, by the fact of the twelve tribes of Israel and the twelve Apostles of Jesus. Perhaps it is significant that it is arrived at by multiplying the earthly number 4 and the spiritual number 3. In this scheme, 5 and 10 are simply "round numbers" or approximations. These are all the numbers that are ever used figuratively by the apocalyptist, though combinations of them frequently occur, as the 1000 years of the millennium, which is the cube of the round number 10, or the 144,000 on Mount Zion, which is the square of the church number 12 multiplied by the cube of the round number 10.

Then there are the figures of *living creatures*, unfortunately often called "beasts" in our English versions. There is the lion, always suggesting strength—strength sometimes used to noble ends, as in the case of Christ who is called the "Lion of the tribe of Judah" (Rev. 5:5), or sometimes the strength of oppression, as in the picture of the Devil as "a roaring lion, seeking some one to devour" (I Peter 5:8). There is the bear, the symbol of stealth; the tiger, suggesting special ferocity; the goat, always the emblem of coarse evil; the lamb, figure of sacrifice; the ox or the calf, symbol of patient service; the eagle, king of birds as the lion is of beasts, and used to portray high flight, usually high spirituality; the face of a man, symbolizing (believe it or not!) intelligence. Often these figures also are seen in composition, as in the case of some dragon that may have the body of a lion and the wings of an eagle, or of some earth-bound creature that has the face of a man but (alas!) the lower portions of some predatory creature.

Perhaps the most interesting of apocalyptic figures are the *colors*. There is white, which is always the symbol of triumph, not necessarily of purity as is sometimes supposed, for the triumph may be that of eternal righteousness or of temporarily powerful evil. There is red, the color of strife, usually of war; black, the color symbolizing famine; "pale," or literally "greenish-gray," the color of a corpse, which symbolizes death; green, the color of eternal life; purple, the symbol of royalty. It is interesting that neither blue nor yellow is used as a symbol in this literature.

There are also *natural portents* which are suggestive of judgment: a darkened (eclipsed) sun, a bloody moon, falling stars. Sometimes these portents become dreadful beyond belief, as in the case of heavens rolled together as a scroll or a bottomless pit opened up under the earth. Earthquakes and cyclonic winds, hail and fire (often mixed together), smoke and ashes, figure in the portraiture of doom. The earth and the sea themselves recur often as symbols—the earth as the seat of man's false religion, the sea as the seat of his false government. Many other figures occur in apocalypses, which are often self-evident, such as the exalted firmament, the throne, the all-seeing eye, the rainbow, harps, seals, and the like. Others, especially precious metals and stones, need special interpretation as one goes along.

There are two general kinds of error which are often made in interpreting apocalyptic figures. On the one hand, people have taken them literally, instead of using them as "signs" as the writers so often bid their readers to do. If taken literally they result, as a rule, in quite poverty-stricken notions of divine activity, such as the limiting of Christ's reign on earth to a thousand years. Or they may suggest frightful notions when joy and peace are intended, as in the case of the throne of God on wheels that are "full of eyes round about" (Ezek. 1:18). Such literalisms have led time and again to needless torturing fears and to false hopes of material changes in the immediate future.

The other type of common error is that which takes the signs figuratively enough but fails to recognize that they are all *symbols*, and never intended to be *images*. Ezekiel's vision of the throne was not meant to be seen with the naked eye; it was intended to convey the impression of God's majesty. The dragon of the Book of Revelation was not intended to be sketched with crayon; he stood for an idea. Forgetful or ignorant of this, men have often placarded hideous pictures before the unsuspecting, such as Doré's illustrations of Milton's *Paradise Lost* or Reubens' famous painting of Napoleon in hell. Such use of symbols as images may serve to affright or to reduce to awe, but they seldom produce that use of inspired imagination which the apocalyptic writer intended.

Apocalyptic Literature Outside the Book of Revelation

As has been hinted, the literature that employs these peculiar figures and that stresses the kind of theology we have outlined is rather bulky. Much of it is found outside our Bible in books that were considered by some to be sacred, by others to be beyond the pale of the Jewish or Christian faith.

Among the apocalypses that are not in our Bible we may single out a few that have apparently had strong influence in Christian thought and may have directly affected the writing of the Book of Revelation. Perhaps the most interesting of them is the Book of Enoch, written not more than two centuries before our Christian era. It is quoted as good authority by one of the New Testament books (Jude 14-15). The biblical character of Enoch, the man who "walked with God" (Gen. 5:22), is represented in the apocryphal book as seeing visions of the fall of the angels, an elaborate development of the story in the sixth chapter of Genesis. In the company of a good angel Enoch journeys to many parts of the earth and even of the underworld to see what the evil angels are doing; he declares God's judgment on them and acts as their advocate in petitioning God for their pardon—a petition which is not granted because of their great vice. In describing the judgment of the angels, Enoch predicts the coming of the "Son of Man" as the judge; he also calls him the "righteous One" and the "Anointed One" (Messiah).

The Assumption of Moses is another book of apocalyptic style, apparently referred to by our Book of Jude (vs. 9). It emphasizes the fight put up by the Devil to secure the body of Moses which God had buried secretly (Deut. 34:5-6). The book brings the story of the world and its evil right down to the days of the Roman Empire in which the Book of Revelation was composed.

Perhaps the work known as the Apocalypse of Baruch will attract many, because it was written at almost exactly the same time as Revelation. Baruch, of course, was another historical character, the scribe of Jeremiah (Jer. 36:4). Following the custom of apocalyptic literature, the writer of this book puts into the mouth of this prophet's servant of the seventh century before Christ a prediction of the fall of Jerusalem—not the destruction by the Babylonians in 587 B.C., but the overthrow by Rome in A.D. 70.

The apocalypse outside our Protestant Bible which most thoroughly resembles Revelation and from which we get our idea of the use of many of its figures is the one known as Fourth Esdras. Like Job, this book deals with the problem of suffering, especially the trials of the persecuted, but it affirms that this problem will never be answered until "the end." The series of visions by which this apocalyptic writer reaches his conclusion involves a great eagle that rose out of the sea (the seat of false human government) with three heads, twelve wings, and some "secondary" wings. The wings turn out to be a succession of rulers who are described in such a way as to make their identification with some of the emperors of Rome inevitable. The vision is quite detailed, but its jargon is carefully explained by an angel, thus giving us extensive clues to the use of apocalyptic symbols.

But one does not need to go outside our Bible to find clear examples of apocalyptic writing. In the Old Testament the outstanding illustration is Daniel, chapters 2 and 7-12. Ezekiel 1 has already been mentioned. Other portions of Ezekiel can probably best be explained as apocalyptic, as can Isaiah 24-27 and Zechariah 12-14. Many would interpret Joel's vision of the "locust" plague in the same general fashion. In the New Testament, we have already referred to the Book of Jude, much of which is reproduced in II Peter. Paul could write in apocalyptic style, as is evidenced by his rhapsody on the return of Christ: I Thessalonians 4:13-18; II Thessalonians 2:1-12. The outstanding apocalypse apart from the Book of Revelation is that which the first three Gospels ascribe to our Lord himself in his discourse concerning the destruction of Jerusalem and the end of the age: Mark 13; Matthew 24; Luke 17:22-37; 21:5-36.

Methods of Interpreting Apocalyptic Literature

Over the years there have been developed several rather well defined methods of interpreting the kind of literature to which the Book of Revelation belongs. These have attained stereotyped names.

Classic Methods

There is the so-called *preterist* interpretation, that is, referring to the past. Those commentators on the Book of Revelation who follow this method entirely, believe that the author is simply reciting, in symbolic form, the story of what has been going on in his lifetime and environment. Such an interpreter thinks of all the nationalistic references in the book as having to do with Rome; he believes that John refers to Rome by his figures of the dragon and the beasts of the sea and the earth. He sees in the Book of Revelation nothing more and nothing less than a cryptographic account of Rome's rise to power and of her fall, with a religious accounting for all that happens and with appropriate warnings and encouragements to the faithful. He is likely to believe also that the book is composed of an older Jewish apocalypse reworked by a Christian hand.

There is next the *historical* method of interpretation. Such interpreters seek to find some point in later history at which the phenomena of the Book of Revelation took place. They may think of the figures of the book as standing for such truths as we have noted, but they claim to be able to locate some era in history during which all the signs used in the book were to be found fulfilled at once, and they are facile at picking out particular characters of history to whom the signs point. Thus, if they can discover some prominent yet evil character whose name, worked out according to some alphabetic code, gives the numerical equivalent of 666, they feel that it was he to whom the writer of the book was referring and they try to find all the other signs in the book "fulfilled" in the days of that evil man. The difficulty with this line of reasoning is that there are so many leading characters of history whose names can be figured out as the equivalent of 666! Protestants have reduced the titles of at least three of the most infamous popes to this figure, and Romanists have pointed with glee to the fact that the Latin form of the name of Martin Luther works out to 666. Some who follow the historical method of interpretation have sought to relieve the difficulty by supposing that the events to which the writer looks forward have recurred several times in history and that he had each occurrence in mind.

Perhaps the best-known method of interpretation is the *futurist*. As its name suggests, those who take this line believe that the writer of the Book of Revelation had in mind events and outcomes that are all still in the future. Though some of them may recognize a historical background in the first century in the case of the letters to the seven churches, they insist that everything else points to a day as yet unrealized. They often look for events that will follow quite literally the sequence of the book. From the futurists have generally come both the "premillennialists" and the "postmillennialists," who see in the prediction of a millennium the wellspring of hope—the one believing that Christ must come in person to the world before that millennium and the other that he will come afterward. (See the comment on chapter 20.) The futurists often include in their group those who figure out according to some number scheme, which they feel they derive from the book, the exact or the approximate date of the end of the world. They have thus spawned many sects that thrive on some quite literal expectation of an "end."

The Apocalyptic Interpretation

The *apocalyptic* interpretation, adopted in this commentary, seeks to preserve the value in each of the other emphases but to go beyond them. With the preterists it recognizes that often the appropriateness of the particular figures used in the Book of Revelation springs from the situation of the days in which it was composed, the days of the Roman Empire that had spread over all the earth. With the historical school it recognizes that situations similar to this recur in history, and that wherever they do take place appropriate reference may be made to the struggles and hopes depicted in this book. With the futurists it sees that much of the dream of this writer is yet to find fruition, and that the Christian faith, like that of the Jews, but unlike most other religions, finds its "golden age" in times that are yet to be. But the apocalyptic interpretation of the Book of Revelation may be said to go beyond all these other methods in that it consistently takes all figures, those of time included, not as literal but as symbolic, and especially in the fact that it interprets the book as a *religious philosophy* of life. By this is meant that the events described in such a work as Revelation are not single events, whether at some point in the past or some hour in the future, but rather that they are the interpretation, under the guise of figures, of how things *always* turn out in this world where evil seems to be in power but where God is actually the unseen Ruler. Given such and such causes, this is the series of results that will follow. Given such and such types of sin, here are the inevitable judgments. Given such and such faithful uses of the "means of grace," here are the triumphs that will ensue.

The Book of Revelation as Biblical Apocalypse

The Book of Revelation has had a rather checkered career in the Canon of our New Testament. For the first two centuries it seems to have been accepted with almost childlike faith and devotion. When in the third century church scholars began to apply rational methods to the interpretation of the Scriptures, some of them questioned Revelation. The great Council of Laodicea, meeting about A.D. 360, left Revelation out of its list of books that were to be read in all the churches. The unfortunate part of the long debate on the place of Revelation in the Canon lies in the fact that when it came back in, accepted by virtually all the Church by the end of the fourth century, it came at a time of prosperity, when apocalyptic was not particularly desired and when the key to its understanding had been allowed to drop out of sight. As a result, Revelation soon became the happy hunting ground of all sorts of fantastic sects with bizarre notions. The Protestant reformers were divided in their ideas about Revelation, Calvin accepting it, Luther relegating it to an "appendix" to the New Testament, Beza, the discoverer of one of the great Greek manuscripts, making use of it, and Erasmus, the editor of an early printed Greek Testament, having his doubts about it. It was not until the middle of the nineteenth century that the Church began again to look at the book for what it is and to understand it in terms of its time and setting.

Author and Date

Who wrote this greatest of all apocalypses? He three times names himself "John" (1:1, 9; 22:8). That this was the Apostle John was devoutly believed in the Early Church. Many of its great leaders are to be numbered among those who credit the book to the Apostle. Others in the Early Church believed it to be an inspired book, written by some other John, such as the often-cited "John the Presbyter" to whom Papias refers in the second century. Students of the book today are likewise divided in their opinions. Some point out how different the book is from the Gospel and the Letters of John, both in style and in dominant line of thought. Others note that certain pictures of the Christ occur in both the Gospel of John and the Apocalypse and are not to be found elsewhere, such as the "Lamb" and the "living water," though the word used for "Lamb" in the Book of Revelation is different from that used in the Gospel of John. Perhaps the most telling argument in favor of the writer's being John the Apostle is the harmony of the teaching of this book with the character of John as he is presented in the Synoptic Gospels. There he is primarily the "son of thunder," and in this book the author believes strongly in the thundering judgments of God. If John could indeed be transformed by Jesus from a son of thunder to an apostle of love, then he might have written both the

Book of Revelation and the Fourth Gospel, for these two compositions are no more in contrast than are the two sides of character represented by these two terms.

Equally in doubt is the date of Revelation. That it was composed during some period of terrible persecution of Christians
by Rome is almost certain. But two such outstanding periods
came to pass in the first century of our Christian era. The first
was the persecution under Nero in the 60's. It is possible that with
this in mind, and with the consciousness that there was more to
come, the author wrote in the late 60's or early 70's. The second
great persecution occurred under Domitian, who reigned A.D. 81-
96, and many interpreters believe that this book stems from that
period, probably from the early 90's. This would allow for the
development in the book of the popular legend of the return of
Nero with its new thrust of spiritual meaning (13:1-4).

OUTLINE

As in the case of most great writing, no one can be certain of just what outline of his thought the author had in mind. Perhaps he wrote under such tension and with such a high degree of inspiration that he was hardly conscious of any logical arrangement of his thought. Yet his work displays marks of careful construction. That it revolves around the repeated number seven is obvious, and many have attempted elaborate reconstructions of the book on the basis of a sevenfold structure from beginning to end. The clue in 1:19 suggests chapters 1-3 as a prelude dealing with Christ's relation to the churches of John's day, "what you see"; chapters 4 and 5 as the glorious basic vision of the worship of God in heaven, "what is"; and the beginning of the cycles of seven at chapter 6 with the story of "what is to take place hereafter." The following outline is a working out of these main divisions.

Introduction. Revelation 1:1-3

The General Letter to the Church. Revelation 1:4-20

The Particular Letters to the Seven Churches. Revelation 2:1—3:22

Worship in Heaven. Revelation 4:1—5:14
   Worship of God as Creator (4:1-11)
   Worship of the Redeeming Lamb (5:1-14)

The Cycle of the Seven Seals. Revelation 6:1—8:5
   The First Six Seals (6:1-17)
   Interlude of the Sealing of the Redeemed (7:1-17)
   The Seventh Seal: Preparation for the New Cycle (8:1-5)

The Cycle of the Seven Trumpets. Revelation 8:6—11:19
   The First Six Trumpets (8:6—9:21)
   Interlude of the Bitter Scroll and the Two Witnesses
      (10:1—11:14)
   The Seventh Trumpet: Announcement of the Impending End
      (11:15-19)

The Cycle of the Seven Mystic Signs. Revelation 12:1—14:20
   The Direct Struggle: the First Three Signs (12:1-17)
   The Indirect Struggle: the Next Three Signs (13:1—14:5)

Interlude of Angelic Messengers and the Blessed Dead
(14:6-13)
The Seventh Sign: the Reaper on the Cloud (14:14-20)

The Cycle of the Seven Bowls. Revelation 15:1—16:21
Preparation for the Pouring of the Bowls (15:1-8)
The First Six Bowls (16:1-12)
Interlude of the Frogs and the Battle of Armageddon
(16:13-16)
The Seventh Bowl: Destruction in the Air (16:17-21)

The Cycle of the Episodes of Final Judgment. Revelation 17:1—
20:15
The Harlot City and the Beast (17:1-18)
Judgment of the Harlot City (18:1-24)
The Hallelujah Chorus (19:1-5)
The Marriage Supper of the Lamb (19:6-10)
The White Horseman (19:11-16)
The Destruction of the Beast and the Prophet (19:17-21)
Interlude of the Millennium, with the Binding and Loosing of
Satan (20:1-10)
The Great White Throne (20:11-15)

The New Heaven and the New Earth. Revelation 21:1—22:5

Conclusion. Revelation 22:6-21

COMMENTARY

INTRODUCTION
Revelation 1:1-3

The Book of Revelation begins with its central figure, Jesus Christ. The opening phrase probably does not mean that Christ is revealed, but that he is revealing God, a revelation which is to be shared with men through "his servant John." Unlike most apocalypses which are "pseudepigraphic," that is, written in the name of another, this book states quite directly what is evidently the name of its actual author. John is to tell of two great realities: God's word and Jesus' testimony to it. He is to tell these mighty truths by bearing "witness" to them. The word used for "witness" here does not mean an onlooker. A witness is one who testifies to what he has seen. And the word here and all through this book is that from which we get our English "martyr."

The blessing given here is threefold, signifying that it comes from the spirit world: first, a blessing on the one who reads this book aloud instead of ignoring it or hiding it (the reference is to the custom of reading Scripture aloud in congregational worship); second, a blessing on those who hear; and third, a blessing on those who "keep" what is written—that is, who use this book in their lives. This is the first of seven beatitudes to be found in the Book of Revelation, the others being at 14:13; 16:15; 19:9; 20:6; 22:7; 22:14. There is also a sense of urgency in the vision: "the time is near." From the standpoint of the apocalyptic writer, "the time" is always near.

THE GENERAL LETTER TO THE CHURCH
Revelation 1:4-20

John, as the agent of Christ, writes his vision in the form of a letter to the Church. It is to the entire Church, represented by the sevenfold group of letters, since seven is the number of that which is complete.

The Greeting (1:4-11)

The Church is saluted, not first by John himself, but from on high (vss. 4-5). Since this greeting is from the spirit world, it is threefold, from each person of the Trinity: from God the Father, described also in threefold fashion, "who is and who was and who is to come," that is, who is eternal; from the Holy Spirit, pictured as "the seven spirits," that is, as the perfect Spirit; and from Jesus Christ, who is here viewed as the "witness," again in the "martyr" sense of the one who gave his life. Such a triune God is the real author of this book. Jesus is himself described in threefold symbolism: not only as the witness, but also as the one raised from the dead, and as the ruler over all the kings of the earth. Thus his sacrifice, his resurrection, and his eternal reign are combined at the very outset. The part played here by the Spirit, as the seven spirits, corresponds fairly closely to the teaching on the Holy Spirit in other portions of the New Testament. The Book of Revelation will be found to be trinitarian throughout, though the persons of the three are not always sharply distinguished.

The ascription of praise to God is another threefold song: "To him who loves us and has freed us . . . and made us . . ." (vss. 5-6). The order of these words is important. It is basically God's love that reaches out to us; his first act is to set us free from sin; but we are set free in order that we may be made into something different from what we were. This is described as "a kingdom, priests . . . ," which probably means "a kingdom *of* priests," involving the double function of royal authority and priestly mediation. It reminds us of the promise of God to Moses concerning Israel, that they should be such a kingdom of priests (Exod. 19:5-6). In the new priesthood made possible by Christ all believers become priests in his presence, a truth which was laid hold of by the Protestant Reformers in the doctrine of the universal priesthood of all believers.

The judgment which the apocalyptist always anticipates is also in this ascription of praise to God—he is "coming with the clouds" (vs. 7)—for this was a common symbol of approaching judgment. The assurance that the judgment will be universal is expressed in the awful sentence, "Every eye will see him, every one who pierced him." This is almost as though those who pierced him would be compelled to look upon his coming. "Alpha" and "Omega" (vs. 8) are the first and last letters of the Greek alphabet; God's timelessness is again emphasized.

John likewise expresses as heavenly in origin the threefold experience which he shares with his readers: "the tribulation and the kingdom and the patient endurance" (vs. 9). One can see how tribulation and patience go together, but to link the Kingdom with them is a triumphant thought that would never occur to the ordinary mind. But it is true that the Kingdom of God itself will be realized only through tribulation and patient endurance. To be "in the Spirit on the Lord's day" (vs. 10) means that the writer felt peculiarly the onset of God's Holy Spirit on the day of the recollection of Jesus' resurrection, the first day of the week.

The "trumpet" voice John hears is the sound that calls to activity in behalf of the victorious Christ. If the reader will look on the map of Asia Minor he will see that the seven churches listed here (vs. 11) are named in the order in which a traveler would reach these seven towns, starting at Ephesus and making a semicircular sweep. This, then, is a circular letter to be read by the sevenfold—that is, the complete—Church.

The Vision of the Son of Man (1:12-20)

What John sees is the most reassuring of all possible visions. The Church, in the seven examples that he takes from Asia, is in the midst of conflict and woe, but the Son of Man is in the midst of the Church! The Church is not itself the light, it is only the lampstand holding up the light (vss. 12, 20). The "angels," or the ministers of the churches, are not themselves the means of the ultimate safety of the Church; they are only as "stars" in the right hand of the Christ (vss. 16, 20). This vision of hope which opens the book centers not in the Church but in the Christ, and not in a Christ who is only at the right hand of power but in the exalted Christ who is also living with his earth-bound Church. Thus both the apocalyptic and the prophetic urgency in the writer are seen in this vision. John pictures, in language often suggestive of the Book of Daniel, three things about the Christ.

1. His *character* (vss. 12-15). John sees him as "one like a son of man," an expression which probably has reference to the glorious figure of Daniel 7:13, the "son of man" who came to the Ancient of Days and received the Kingdom from his hand. This glorified figure of the Son of Man has innate dignity, represented by the long robe; he is priestly, as seen in the girdle at his breast (the king wore his girdle at the waist); he is abundantly wise, as pictured in the full head of white hair (a symbol of the wisdom of age); he is discerning in judgment, as noted in the

flaming or piercing eyes; he is triumphant over his foes, as stressed in the feet of refined bronze; his voice is varied and powerful, like the sound or rush of many waters, an expression which an earlier prophet had used of God (Ezek. 43:2).

2. His *ministry* (vss. 16-17a). The work of the Son of Man in the midst of his Church is here pictured as a combination of preservation and judgment. The judgment is seen in the two-edged sword, which he does not carry as a defensive instrument but which proceeds out of his mouth; it is his word which judges men. His face is as brilliant with his judgment as the sun when it shines at full strength. But at the same time there is gracious ministry to his own, for he holds the seven stars (later defined as the "angels" or perhaps the pastors of the seven churches) in his right hand. And yet, logically impossible as it would be, in the vision that same right hand is laid on the prostrated John to lift him up in renewed life. It is as though the writer would say, "The hand of Christ is never so filled with concern for the whole church but that he can lay it strengtheningly on the weakened individual."

3. His *resources* (vss. 17b-18). It is worth noting how carefully the author authenticates his central figure at the beginning of his writing. The first question that would naturally arise about one for whom this book makes such lavish claims is this: What is he like? What sort of person is he? So John describes his character first. Then one would want to know, What can he do with such a character? Is it simply a marvel or is it useful? And so John makes clear his ministry. But about anyone whose outstanding person and work are so magnificent the doubt might well arise, Can he hold out? Is he just a "flash in the pan" or does he possess lasting qualities? And so it is that John closes his vision of the Christ in the midst of his Church by picturing his everlasting resources, his unfailing grace and power.

Christ can draw upon the powers of his eternal life: "I am the first and the last, and the living one." He can also draw on the latent power that resides in his victory over death. It is because he both died and is alive that he has the power of "Death and Hades," or, as we would say, death and the grave.

Verse 19 is really the key to the organization of the book. John is bidden to write, "what you see" (or, more literally, "what you have seen"), which is the condition of the Church as pictured in chapters 2 and 3; "what is," which refers to the glorious vision of

God and the Lamb in chapters 4 and 5; "what is to take place hereafter," which is revealed in the remainder of the book.

THE PARTICULAR LETTERS TO THE SEVEN CHURCHES
Revelation 2:1—3:22

The Church as a whole has been first encouraged to know that it does not stand alone in the world of tribulation, that the glorified Son of Man stands in its midst. Now the reality of that general vision is applied to the churches in particular. For that purpose the seven churches of Asia Minor are selected for specific examination, since they form the writer's parish from which he has been separated by banishment to Patmos. This rocky island lay in the Aegean Sea off the coast of Asia Minor, some seventy-five miles southwest of Ephesus. On a clear day the exiled writer could probably see the outline of the mainland where thrived the cities he loved so well to serve. The seven churches named here are, of course, not the only particular congregations that existed in Asia Minor in John's day, but they are chosen as typical of the Church at large. There is a certain parallelism about the particular letters. In most of them there is stated some special factor in their situation that God knows and understands. The good that is in the church is picked out for praise. Some pet sin that is being harbored in the church is then brought to light. The church is called on to repent and usually is told just how it needs to repent. And best of all, there is applied to each particular example some one of the qualities of the character or the ministry or the resources of the Son of Man that are pictured in the first chapter—some part of them that this individual church especially needs. If one wished to make a chart of these various parts of each of these seven letters and if he desired to be alliterative so as to help his memory, he might say that John features in each church seven things: its Location, Commendation, Condemnation, Vocation, Application (of the Christ), Exhortation, and Remuneration. Occasionally one of these is left out of a letter: there is no condemnation of the church at Smyrna or of that at Philadelphia, and no commendation of the church at Laodicea. But the application of some quality of the Christ to each is always there, and that is most important of all.

In all these letters there is the background of the old prophetic doctrine of the *remnant,* represented in each church by those who "conquer." The writer apparently has no hope that all the people, even within a given church, will turn from evil to the true way of God, but he does expect that through the grace and power of the Christ in their midst there will always be a remnant. But he cautions even this remnant that it will not be saved unless it bestirs itself. "He who has an ear . . ." recurs in all the letters and reminds us of Jesus' own repeated warning to those who listened to his parables (for example, Mark 4:9).

That these letters are filled with figures drawn from the religious myths of other lands is often pointed out by scholars. Especially is this the case with the use of Babylonian astrology. Yet the important issues are not the "stars" or other astral objects, but the Christ who is far beyond the reach of ancient mythology and who is the center of life for his Church.

The Letter to Ephesus (2:1-7)

John begins with the great capital of Asia Minor. Situated near the coast, it was a center of trade both by land and by sea. One of its most lucrative industries was the manufacture of idols and other articles for the worshipers at the temple of Artemis which dominated its life (Acts 19:21-41). Ephesus was apparently the seat of many sects, both without and within the Church, among which were the "Nicolaitans" whom John mentions (vs. 6) and about whom we know little. It is significant that this church is commended for rooting out heresies and without weariness rejecting each of them as it arises (vss. 2-3). Yet at the same time this church is condemned for having abandoned the love it had at first (vs. 4). Perhaps the two go together! It is hard to keep the eye wary for all forms of evil, however necessary that may be, and keep love in full glow at the same time. Yet a strong hope is held out for Ephesus. Though it has not kept its love, there is applied to it, from the vision in the first chapter, the Christ of the keeping power "who holds the seven stars in his right hand" (vs. 1), and it is promised the "tree of life" (vs. 7). The reference here to the Garden of Eden is unmistakable. It is as though the author had said, "Before there were any heresies among God's people you lived in the garden of his favor. But when you sinned, you were cast out lest you eat of the tree of eternal life while you were sinning and become

immortal in your sin. But now you who conquer evil have the
gift of Christ which is life eternal, and so you may eat of the tree
of life and be admitted to God's new paradise."

The Letter to Smyrna (2:8-11)

To this church John's letter is entirely one of sympathy and
encouragement; there is no incriminating evidence to be brought
against the Christians. That they were the center of poverty and
persecution is evident (vs. 9). That the enmity was Jewish in
origin made it all the harder to bear, and it is not surprising that
John, in keeping with his general theology, lays the blame at the
door of Satan who has stirred them up to evil. John expects much
worse persecution still to come on this church, and instead of
describing it as enduring for the limited period of three and a
half days, as he might be expected to do, he pictures it as suffering a rounded-out tribulation of "ten days" (vs. 10; see Introduction). Yet some of the richest of blessings are pronounced on
the Smyrna church. Here occurs the wondrous promise to those
who do not flinch: "Be faithful unto death, and I will give you
the crown of life" (vs. 10). To this church is applied the gift of
Christ who himself died and came to life (vs. 8), and it is promised escape from the "second death," which is the spiritual death
of separation from God (vs. 11).

The Letter to Pergamum (2:12-17)

Here was a city where it was hard indeed to maintain a Christian church. The seat of emperor worship for its district, it is described as the place "where Satan's throne is" (vs. 13). Already
faithfulness to Christ had cost the life of at least one disciple
here, Antipas, about whom we know nothing else. Although
John commends the people who hold fast in such a situation, he
condemns the immorality he finds there.

Jewish writings had added much legend to the story of Balaam.
In the Bible itself Balaam is pictured simply as the prophet who
wanted to lie about Israel to Balak king of Moab in order to ob-
tain the rich gifts he offered as a reward, but who felt constantly
forced to speak the true word God gave him about Israel's coming
triumph over the Moabites (Num. 22-24). The Jews apparently
were not a little nettled by this record of one who would have
cursed them if he could, and they conjured up all sorts of stories
about his teaching flagrant immoralities to the people. So John

uses this story of Balaam to picture figuratively the gross evils
that had crept into the church at Pergamum, evils which he seems
to have identified with those of the Nicolaitans who are mentioned here again (vss. 14-15). It is quite appropriate that the
Christ of the first chapter who is applied to this church should be
the one with the sword in his mouth, judging evil sharply (vs.
12). But it is also in keeping that to the penitent should be promised the purity of a new name written on the white stone (vs. 17),
for in ancient times the white stone was greatly prized, either as
an amulet, especially if the name of some deity was engraved
upon it, or as a mark of membership in a special group. And the
white color of course suggests victorious living.

The Letter to Thyatira (2:18-29)

Here is another church that needs a housecleaning, and the
Christ of the flaming eyes and the feet of bronze is brought to
bear upon it (vs. 18). Gentile practices, especially gross per-
version of natural morality, were common here, and another Old
Testament character is used to symbolize such evil (vs. 20).
"Jezebel" is probably not the actual name of any woman in the
church, but a figurative way of saying that they have a woman
teacher who is as beguiling as was the Sidonian princess of this
name who led Israel astray (see I Kings 18:13, 19; 21:1-16). At
greater length than in most of the other letters, the writer draws
out the description of her punishment in language appropriate to
her kind of sin, which seems to have been a combination of fleshly
and spiritual wrongs (vss. 20-23). The warning against the "deep
things of Satan" (vs. 24) must have been particularly timely. It
is somewhat difficult to see the appropriateness of the autocratic
rule promised here to the victors over evil (vss. 26-27). The
words are reminiscent of Psalm 2, verses 8 and 9, and they probably suggested to John the ability to crush sensuality. More to
our liking is the final part of the promise, that of "the morning
star" (vs. 28), a gift which suggests the freshness and purity that
were so evidently needed by this church.

The Letter to Sardis (3:1-6)

Unlike the first church in this series, that in Ephesus, the
church at Sardis was deteriorating in its works. In fact, it was
actually dead while sustaining a reputation for being alive (vss.
1-2). Keenly pertinent is the writer's warning that to the church

which drifts along, thinking itself to be what it is not, Christ comes like a thief (vs. 3)—a reminiscence of the Master's own warning (Luke 12:39). Since this church is actually dead, it has no spirit of its own; hence the Christ of the first chapter who is applied to its need is the one who had the perfect Spirit, that is, the seven spirits (vs. 1). The promise is again a new purity, this time prefigured as white garments, together with a name retained in the book of life (vs. 5). The encouragement to believe that if they do not deny Christ he will actually confess them before his Father as his very own is based on Jesus' words to his disciples (Matt. 10:32).

The Letter to Philadelphia (3:7-13)

Behold the city of the "open door," the church of opportunity! (vs. 8). No wonder the Christ who is applied to it is the Christ of the keys, who can both shut and open. The writer's purpose seems to be to warn the church not to fail to enter while the door remains ajar. Again certain Jews are called the synagogue of Satan (vs. 9), even as they were in the letter to Smyrna (2:9). Again there is the urgency to hold fast, but this time the ground for such admonition is the expectancy that Christ will soon come to them and thus relieve their suffering (vs. 11). Here is a church without blame, if only it lets no one seize its crown (vs. 11). It is in the process of preparation for being "a pillar" in God's temple (vs. 12). The most delightful promise of all these letters is included here: that of the three names (vs. 12). No essential difference is intended between "the name of my God," "the name of the city of my God," and "my own new name," but the characteristic threefold way of putting this pledge is most inviting. "Name" denotes character, and the believer who remains true may contemplate his character made into the likeness of God's holy city— yes, of the character of Christ, and even of that of God himself.

The Letter to Laodicea (3:14-22)

This last of the letters introduces us to a church that evokes no words of praise. Because this chances to come last, it has been thought by some to point to the fact that the Church will decline through a series of ages, beginning with the age of the Ephesian church and coming on down to this one at Laodicea. But these churches were all contemporaries of the writer; one of the best churches in this group is that at Philadelphia, which immediately precedes this one. No scale, either descending or ascending, is intended, but only the laying bare of the life of all phases of the Church before the eyes of him with whom we have to do.

The church at Laodicea was rich (vs. 17). It was situated in the wealthy Lycus River valley, where was also the Pauline church of Colossae. It is said that when an earthquake destroyed these cities, their inhabitants rebuilt them with holdings that they had elsewhere and without aid from other people. But, as so often happens, a religious group that waxes rich becomes self-sufficient and then indifferent. And John rightly discerns that God cannot stand indifference as well as he can outright sinfulness (vs. 15). So he pictures the Laodicean church as lukewarm water which is brackish and which one spews out of his mouth (vs. 16). The church is admonished to realize that it is actually poor in spirituality and that it needs to buy of God the gifts that cannot be purchased with money (vss. 17-18). Often quoted is the assurance, "Behold, I stand at the door and knock" (vs. 20). In its setting, of course, this means that Christ is knocking at the door of the church. If we keep this meaning, the promise that follows is all the more remarkable: "If any one hears my voice and opens the door, I will come in to him . . ."; that is, even when Christ is knocking at the closed door of such an uncaring church as that at Laodicea, an individual may still open the door of the church, and if he does, Christ will come in and fellowship—at least with that individual. Great boon for the warmhearted remnant in a cold church! No wonder the picture of Christ applied to them is that of the "faithful and true witness" (vs. 14), and that the promise is the mighty throne of Christ itself (vs. 21).

Thus the letters to the seven churches express a pastoral concern both for the Church as a whole and for the needs of particular groups of those who are in Christ. The writer is a sufferer himself, one who is enduring the trials of persecution by the state, and so he is particularly mindful of those who suffer in like manner for their faith. He is fearful lest some of them will give up that faith rather than suffer still more for it. He is honest; he does not try to entice his people to steadfastness by the promise that the worst is over. Indeed he often pictures more terrible persecutions in the offing. Christians of all ages, our own included, have known what it means to suffer for their faith—sometimes at the direction of an oppressive and suspicious government, sometimes at the dictates of an economic order that is flagrantly unchristian,

sometimes from the spite of those whose social customs are dearer
to them than the love of God, sometimes even at the hand of their
own family who have turned against them because of their lofty
way of life. In every such case, the emphasis must be what it is in
these letters: not on success, but on faithfulness; not on human
resources, whether of military defense or of personal strength, but
on the Christ who is sufficient for every need. For John found, as
Paul found before him, and as every loyal follower in every age
must find, that Christ's "power is made perfect in weakness" (II
Cor. 12:9).

WORSHIP IN HEAVEN
Revelation 4:1—5:14

One of the most attractive points of style in the Book of Revelation is its alternation between scenes in heaven and scenes on
earth. The apocalypse opened with a glorious picture of the
exalted Son of Man, a revealing of the eternal Christ in all his
essential deity and power. There followed the scene on earth of
the persecuted and almost frustrated churches, though this black
and white drawing was relieved in each case by the application of
grace and strength from this same Son of Man. Now we are returned to the heavenly courts for a beatific scene of worship, where
much of the detail work reminds us of such Old Testament passages as Isaiah 6, Daniel 7, and Ezekiel 1 and 10. Actually there
are two scenes: the worship of God as creator, which is the theme
of chapter 4, and the worship of Christ as redeemer, which illu-
mines chapter 5. From these two scenes, especially from the figures used, issue most of the action of the remainder of the book.
Prophecy, in its fullest and richest sense, springs from the worship of God.

Worship of God as Creator (4:1-11)

"In heaven an open door!" (vs. 1). Even though, in the spirit
of an apocalypse, this book emphasizes the transcendence of God,
it pictures no cold removal of God from men. John is invited to
come into God's very presence and to gaze upon the many acts
of worship in heaven; in fact, he is summoned by a trumpet voice.
That the herald should describe the worship scene as "what must
take place after this" shows again the close connection in the writ-

er's mind between heaven and earth. That the "one seated on the throne" is not named (vs. 2) contributes to the awesomeness of the scene. The "jasper" stone (vs. 3) suggests translucence, and hence may have been more like our opal, brilliant in color. It had been part of the galaxy of precious stones in the high priest's breastplate (Exod. 28:20). The "carnelian" is a deep red, suggesting fire. The emerald rainbow, of course, is the mark of promise. The heavenly court surrounds the Almighty (vs. 4). The twenty-four elders on thrones suggest power secondary to that of God, the twenty-four probably representing the twelve tribes of Israel and the twelve Apostles of Christ. That they are "clad in white garments" signifies that they have come off victorious in conflict, and the "golden crowns," that they are now worthy to reign with God. The storm that issues from the throne (vs. 5) is symbolic of judgment that proceeds from God, and the "seven spirits" denote again the perfect Holy Spirit. The throne itself can be seen from underneath, since it rests on "a sea of glass" (vs. 6).

As in the case of Ezekiel's vision of the wheels of the chariot on high (Ezek. 1), there surround God's throne "living creatures" who are carefully pictured and who, since they are four in number, represent the earth (vss. 6-8). They have eyes on all sides; that is, they see all that is going on in all directions. They have the qualities we have listed as belonging to the living creatures of other apocalypses: the lion of strength, the ox of service, the man of intelligence, and the eagle of high spiritual flight. Like Isaiah's seraphim (Isa. 6), each has six wings, in this case these being equipped also with all-seeing eyes, and like them they sing continually the hymn of the triple holiness of God whose might is here pictured as eternal—past, present, and future. It will be well worth while to read this fourth chapter of Revelation and the sixth chapter of Isaiah together and then go carefully through the hymn, "Holy, holy, holy, Lord God Almighty," noting how remarkably the hymnist has blended the figures used by Isaiah and John.

Worship rises to its peak as the four living creatures honor the spiritual nature of God by ascribing to him graces in the spiritual number of three—"glory and honor and thanks" (vs. 9)—while the twenty-four elders complete the picture by casting their crowns before the throne and leading the grand paean of worship (vss. 10-11). This final burst of praise also is in three parts—

"glory and honor and power"—and is sung to the greatness and eternity of God's creatorship.

Worship of the Redeeming Lamb (5:1-14)

Closely integrated with the adoration of God is the new worship that is called forth. In God's right hand there is the scroll, the book of destiny (vs. 1), reminding us somewhat of the scroll Ezekiel saw (Ezek. 2:9-10). But this one is far more momentous. It is sealed with seven seals, that is, completely sealed, and no one can be found to open it (vss. 2-4). It is of note that John plays on the two qualities needed in one able to unroll the scroll—worthiness and power. Both must be combined in one person. The scroll is apparently so arranged that one seal can be broken at a time and a portion of it unrolled, but only by one who is both powerful enough and worthy enough.

The literary device of having the seer weep because he cannot fathom the mystery is common in apocalyptic literature, but here it is not for long, as he is soon pointed to the conqueror who is both "Lion" and "Root" in the spiritual house of David (vs. 5); that is, one who is the very source of strength. But the beauty and glory of the scene lie in its marvelous combination of impossible opposites. John looks for the "Lion," emblem of strength, and he sees a "Lamb," symbol of weakness and of sacrificial offering. Yet it is the fact that he has been sacrificed that makes this Lamb so strong that he can open the scroll (vss. 6-7), for the Lamb is "standing, as though it had been slain"; that is, the Passover Lamb is living! This is literally inconceivable, of course, but spiritually the greatest truth in the universe: the power to stand and to take the book of judgment and break its hard-set seals belongs to the Christ who has been sacrificed and who has overcome the power of death.

This is perhaps the most important figure of the Book of Revelation. None but an inspired composer of heavenly visions would ever have thought of it. When earth-bound men want symbols of power they conjure up mighty beasts and birds of prey. Russia elevates the bear, Britain the lion, France the tiger, the United States the spread eagle—all of them ravenous. It is only the Kingdom of Heaven that would dare to use as its symbol of might, not the Lion for which John was looking, but the helpless Lamb, and at that, a slain Lamb—yet one that could stand even after it had been slain. Thus does the "foolishness of God" put to nought the "wisdom of men"! John uses this figure of the mighty Lamb more than two dozen times in his short book (see, for example, 6:16; 7:9; 14:1).

The familiar apocalyptic figures occur again in this vision. The Lamb has "seven horns" (vs. 6) denoting complete power, and "seven eyes," which are the perfect and seeing Spirit. When the Lamb takes the sealed scroll from the hand of God, elders and living creatures alike fall down before him in worship, presenting instruments of praise, "each holding a harp," and symbolic signs of prayers, "golden bowls full of incense" (vss. 7-8). These prayers are said to be those of "the saints." This probably does not mean those still on earth, but those martyred saints whom we are to meet shortly, in chapter 6. The song that is sung is again one of worthiness, the worth won by Christ's shedding the ransoming blood (vs. 9). The ancient priests had taught that "it is the blood that makes atonement, by reason of the life" (Lev. 17:11); that is, the life is in the blood, and therefore the shedding of blood symbolizes the giving of life. That the ransoming of men is not limited to Jews but is for men of all the earth is represented in the earth number four, "men . . . from every tribe and tongue and people and nation." But that the redeeming Lamb makes these ransomed ones spiritual is symbolized by the number three: he has made them to be a kingdom and priests and reigners (vs. 10).

Then follows the mightiest chorus of them all (vss. 11-12): "Worthy is the Lamb who was slain." Seven ascriptions of praise are made to him, for he is the perfect redeemer. Then from heaven and earth, and below the earth and even in the sea—four places—hymns of worship rise both to God, "him who sits upon the throne," and to "the Lamb," with their fourfold ascription because it comes from men of earth (vs. 13). The final act of worship is reserved for the twenty-four elders and the final "Amen!" for the four living creatures who surround the throne (vs. 14).

THE CYCLE OF THE SEVEN SEALS
Revelation 6:1—8:5

The nature of the cycle in the Book of Revelation becomes quite plain in the awesome atmosphere in which the Lamb opens each of the seven seals. There are two groups of these seals: the four and the three. The first four affect the earth directly. The other three take us, as they are unrolled, to the spirit world—in this case the good spirit world of heaven.

The First Six Seals (6:1-17)

The First Four Seals: Judgment on the Earth (6:1-8)

Since it is the scroll of destiny that the Lamb is opening, we are not surprised that judgment issues from the cycle of the seals, and since it is the earth and earthly men who are most immediately affected by judgment, we could expect also that the first four of the seals will have to do with judgment on the earth. And so they do. They take the form of four horsemen riding forth over the earth, following one upon another as in procession. This means that the four are in spiritual sequence and so must all have to do with the same general purpose. That purpose is determined by the color of their horses: white, red, black, and "pale," or greenish-gray—this last word, in the original, is that from which our "chlorine" comes. These colors, as noted in the Introduction, suggest in turn victorious conquest, war, famine, and death. Hence, since the war, famine, and death are destined outcomes from the conquering, the "white" here must be the victory, not of purity, but of selfish, lustful conquest.

This will be a surprise and disappointment to some. The white horseman of verse 2 is often interpreted as referring to Christ, and the fact that he is pictured as "coming" is thought to refer to his second advent. In support of this it is pointed out that the white horseman who comes at 19:11 is obviously Christ; indeed he is named "The Word of God" (19:13). But, as we noted in the Introduction, white is the color of victory, whether it be of good or evil. We are not ready as yet, in this apocalypse, for the triumph of the good conqueror, Christ; we must first be realists enough to face the temporary triumphs of evil forces. That they are evil is manifest from the sequence: the rider on the white horse goes forth "conquering and to conquer" (vs. 2); there follows one on a "bright red" horse who "was permitted to take peace from the earth" and he had a "great sword" (vs. 4); the rider on the black horse "had a balance [or scales] in his hand" (vs. 5), signifying the scarcity of food; the rider on the "pale" horse is definitely named "Death" (vs. 8). When Jesus Christ comes to men he does not bring these powers of destruction—war and famine and death. He comes that men "may have life, and have it abundantly" (John 10:10).

It is now possible to see in concrete fashion what was meant by saying earlier that there is usually a preterist situation—that is, one that is past, one that existed in John's day—which gives appropriateness to the figure. But it also becomes clear that the important point is not whether we can figure out exactly what this situation was or can agree on it as background. It is the philosophy of life, the spiritual order of the world as taught in these symbols, that is vital and that recurs again and again. In the present instance, John uses the horseman with the bow, probably to distinguish him from Roman armies which fought with heavier weapons. Most scholars see in this figure the suggestion of a Parthian invasion, for the Romans often used some Parthian horde to ravish a land which was rebellious. The Parthians were noted bowmen, and so the general background would fit. But this is not the point to stress, and this is the reason we cannot read the Book of Revelation as only an account of doings in the first century of our Christian era. John is dealing with a more far-reaching outlook. The real concern is that whenever any individual or any nation decides on a career of conquest, that nation or person leaves in his train desolation and death. This truth must be preached over and over from the Book of Revelation in each succeeding generation, for each age tends to produce those who do this very thing. If Russia or the United States or any other nation starts out on a career of aggression, it can end in only one way—in war and famine and death. The same thing happens whenever an individual starts out to dominate his family or his business, his neighborhood or his church: conflict and desolation result. Only Christ can conquer and leave good, for only Christ is pure.

Nevertheless there is mercy in such a judgment, because of the goodness of God. In the opening of the third seal, the damage is to be limited to the grains; the "oil and wine" are not to be touched. In the case of the fourth seal, it is only a "fourth" of the earth on which death and destruction are visited. This is a view of partial judgment accomplished, not at any one period of time, but over and over again in this world, whenever men's natural sequence of selfish lusts is allowed to work itself out. Men bring their own judgment on themselves by their own uncontrolled desires, and even though the grace of God spares some, desolation is widespread.

The Fifth Seal: Vision of the Martyred Saints (6:9-11)

As is generally true in the cycles of seven, the first four have
to do with the earth and the other three with the spirit world. In
this case it is the spirit world of heaven. We are transported in
mind to the abode of God where we see an altar, similar to that
in the earthly temple. That the souls of those who were slain on
earth for their faith are now "under the altar" seems to suggest
at once their safety in the keeping of God and also their position
as a sacrifice. They have been killed on earth, but they are thought
of as being offered upon God's own altar (vs. 9). That they cry
for judgment on the earthly foes responsible for their fate (vs.
10) is quite natural, though it represents one of the points at
which the theology of apocalyptic does not rise as high as that
of other biblical theology. It is not of the same spirit as Jesus' cry
on the cross for the forgiveness of his enemies (Luke 23:34) or
even of Stephen's quiet prayer that his death be not held against
his persecutors (Acts 7:60). Still, it must not be forgotten that
in all times when persecution is severe, the martyr very naturally
becomes the symbol of the life completely given to God. In any
age the Christian is to be able to say with Paul, "I do not account
my life of any value nor as precious to myself" (Acts 20:24).
God's long view of time, so often emphasized in the Bible, again
leads to the assurance that the martyrs wear white robes (the
symbol of their victory) and that they need wait only "a little
longer" until the sum total of all martyrs is complete (vs. 11).

The Sixth Seal: The Wrath of the Lamb (6:12-17)

The mighty display of judgment which this seal pictures comes
direct from heaven itself. It is framed in scenes of natural portents which are ever the apocalyptist's figures for such judgment.
If one is tempted here to be a literalist and to imagine that the
writer is thinking of some one time in history when these awful
phenomena have occurred, let him remember that such figures
are used often in Scripture of the day of God's wrath on some
particular people, as in Isaiah 34:4 and Joel 2:10. If one were
to take literally the great earthquake that destroys the earth at this
point, he would have difficulty with the later scenes in Revelation
where the earth is again shaken by God to its very foundations
(Rev. 8:5; 11:13; 16:18). The point on which to concen-
trate here is the paradox of a Lamb filled with such wrath that

the very heavens and earth bow in devastating terror before his face and the people of earth call for the worst horrors of the universe to overtake them rather than be forced to face the Savior's ire. If such a figure gives trouble, let all Christians remember that just because the love of God in Christ is so gracious and so self-giving and so far-seeking, it becomes the most potent force for judgment in all the world when it is rejected.

Interlude of the Sealing of the Redeemed (7:1-17)

As is usual in the cycles of seven in the Book of Revelation, when one reads the sixth he feels that the end of all things is at hand. What, for instance, could be more final than the devastation just pictured in the sixth seal? Yet, as is also usual in this book, between the sixth and seventh of any cycle there occurs an interlude, and the interlude is in two parts. In this case there is pictured the sealing of the redeemed, and the two portions are the redeemed of Israel and the redeemed of the Gentiles.

None of the fury of the Lamb's wrath is to be spent until those who have yielded to his love have been "sealed . . . upon their foreheads" (vss. 1-3). There is another vision involved here, that of "four angels standing at the four corners of the earth" (vs. 1), ready to loose the winds of fate but holding them back until the sealing is complete. The sealing of the redeemed out of Israel is pictured in a very formal symbol, the "hundred and forty-four thousand" (vss. 4-8), which is the square of the church number twelve, multiplied by the cube of the round number ten, and so it indicates no exact figure, but rather the complete number who shall come to God out of Israel. The number is further broken down into twelve groups, representing the twelve tribes of Israel, although the list of those tribes given here is different from that found in any other part of the Bible. It is impossible to say why this particular listing occurs, although it may be significant that the tribe of Judah, from which Christ came in the flesh, is placed ahead of the tribe of Reuben, Jacob's first-born.

Far more beautiful is the second part of the interlude, where the "great multitude" of the redeemed taken from "every nation, from all tribes and peoples and tongues"—four sources again— are sealed. In both cases, apparently, the sealing marks the redeemed as God's own and stresses the safety of those who are possessed by God. That the great multitude is a victorious throng is emphasized once again by the white robes and also by palm branches in their hands (vs. 9). They join the sevenfold song of perfect praise to God (vs. 12). Note the reappearance of the figures of chapters 4 and 5: God and the Lamb to whom are ascribed salvation (vs. 10); the elders and the four living creatures before the throne (vs. 11). The picture is completed by a typical conversation between the seer and an elder, in which the seer does not understand the simplest meaning until he is told (vss. 13-14).

The exceeding beauty of this last scene (vss. 13-17) embraces some of the finest poetry and some of the grandest theology of this book. That the safety of God's redeemed is in their coming out of great tribulation and washing their robes in the blood of the Lamb, that they are sheltered by God who sits on his throne, that they neither hunger nor thirst nor suffer the scorching heat of the desert, and that all tears are wiped away—these are the eternal tokens of God's goodness that have comforted Christians of all ages as they look forward, through whatever means of death, to the great Beyond.

But attention should also be riveted on two remarkable figures that are often overlooked in this passage. The redeemed are said to "serve him day and night within his temple" (vs. 15). Life with God is not pictured by the apocalyptist as one of ease and idleness; it is one in which the service begun here on earth reaches its highest fulfillment (see also 22:3).

The other note of noble theology is that found in the last verse of this chapter. Again we have a figure that is literally impossible: "the Lamb . . . will be their shepherd." How can a lamb turn into a shepherd? But that is just the writer's point: it is Christ, who as the sacrificial Lamb experienced all the sufferings of the flock, who becomes the sympathetic Shepherd guiding that flock. Moreover, it is the Lamb "in the midst of the throne," again a paradox; for one could not literally think of a lamb's becoming a king. But as this Lamb of God becomes the Shepherd of the redeemed, so he also becomes their ruler, while still retaining the properties of the suffering and understanding Lamb.

The Seventh Seal: Preparation for the New Cycle (8:1-5)

It is still the Lamb who is opening the seals, even though this one portends new judgments. Mingled with the smoke of the in-

cense of many prayers are the contents of the censer which an
angel fills from off God's altar and throws upon the earth. That
we are going back from heaven to earth for the next scene is
emphasized by the four again: "peals of thunder, loud noises,
flashes of lightning, and an earthquake." We are thus introduced
to the first four of the next cycle, that of the trumpets.

The delicate sensitivity of the apocalyptist's plot for his great
drama should be noted here. All seven of the trumpets proceed
from the opening of the seventh seal; that is, the complete new
cycle is involved in the one which has gone before. Verily, this
is true to life as history reveals it to us!

THE CYCLE OF THE SEVEN TRUMPETS
Revelation 8:6—11:19

The First Six Trumpets (8:6—9:21)

The First Four Trumpets and the Earth (8:6-12)

As with the cycle of the seven seals, so with the trumpets: they
fall into two groupings, the four and the three. Again the four
deal with judgment as it concerns the earth. But while the first
four seals with their parade of horsemen represent judgment as
following naturally upon the selfish graspings of men, the first
four trumpets announce that God is directly bringing judgment.

Each angel in turn blows his trumpet, and announcement of
the result is made. In each case some part of the earth or human
life upon the earth is affected. The similarity of these scourgings
to the plagues God brought on Egypt in the time of Moses is
evident (Exod. 7-11). Once more the judgment is only partial,
as was the case with the woes let loose by the four horsemen.
The blowing of the first trumpet proclaims calamity on a third
of the earth and a third of the trees and all green grass—though
why "all" in the case of the grass instead of only a third can
hardly be seen. The second trumpet announces the hurling of a
flaming mountain into the sea with the attending destruction of
a third of all that is in the sea. The flourish of the third trumpet
brings down to earth a great falling star whose name is declared
to be "Wormwood," that is, poison. A falling star is the symbol
of a fallen personality. Who the devastating personality of John's
day might have been we can only guess, but it is significant that

his poison pollutes a third of the waters which are the very well-spring of life. While the voice of the fourth trumpet blasts forth the notice that a third of sun and moon and stars have been darkened, it is not the effect of this upon the heaven, but rather the withdrawing of their light from the earth that is the point of the writer's interest. Hence this trumpet joins with the others of the first four in proclaiming judgment upon earth.

The long-range religious thought that lies behind these figures is rich with scriptural truth. The four horsemen of the seals have made plain one vantage point from which God's judgments may be viewed. All God needs to do is to leave men alone in their crime and their sins will work out their own judgment. Greedy conquest, the seeking to get what is not ours, leads always to war and famine and death. But the trumpets have proclaimed the fact that God does not always leave men to their own devices. Sometimes he punishes with terrible scourges the children of men, but always with the purpose (as John will make clear later) of trying to bring them to their senses and win them back to himself. And it is not that the one kind of judgment follows the other in point of time. God does not necessarily let men work out their own affairs first and then step in. The trumpets are not at some later point of time in the world's history than the seals. Both of these kinds of judgment are going on all the time. Yet the four trumpets come out of the seals, with the recognition that God's own judgments on mankind are really just what man's own sins have made inevitable. Such a philosophy of the outcome of life is part of the Christian message.

The Fifth Trumpet and the Spirit World of Evil (8:13—9:11)

As in the case of the last three seals, the last three trumpets take the reader to the spirit world; but while in the former instance it was the good spirit world of heaven, the blowing of the last three trumpets announces the linkage of the evil world of hell with the earth. As a prelude to these awful scenes, the voice of an eagle is heard in mid-heaven announcing these last three trumpets in terms of "woes," that is, curses (8:13).

Another fallen star, which suggests another debased personality (perhaps in John's thought a fallen angel), introduces hell to earth by taking a key and opening "the shaft of the bottomless pit." The evil creatures that are let forth in the smoke that rises from the pit are not to bring scourges on nature as we saw happening in the case of the first four trumpets, but are to attack men themselves—all evil men "who have not the seal of God upon their foreheads" (9:3-4), that is, those who do not belong to God. These evil creatures are called "locusts." They have the power of scorpions (vs. 3), and the torture of their sting is so great that men will seek death as a relief even though God has held back from these monsters the power to inflict death (vss. 5-6). The only mercy shown is in the fact that the scourge is to last "five months," half of ten—that is, a limited and incomplete time.

That locusts were fitting symbols of judgment to all who had lived in the writer's part of the world is well known. Their ability to come up suddenly in such droves as to darken the sun and destroy vegetation and other sources of life was a reality. The prophet Joel had used them as his symbol of the "day of the LORD" (Joel 1:1-7; 2:1-11). But so terrible was a plague of locusts that writers with imagination could not stop with any prosaic account of them. Joel had used the locusts apocalyptically to picture the end of all things, and in so doing he had vested them with all kinds of weird forms, making of them an army in full battle array. So also here, John describes the locusts with lurid fancy (9:7-11). They look like battle steeds; they have human hair, but long, like the hair of women; their teeth are like lions' teeth; their scales are huge as breastplates; their sound is like the noise of rushing chariots; their tails have a venomous sting. And most grotesque of all: their home in the bottomless pit is presided over by a fallen angel, called "Apollyon," that is, "Destroyer."

Such a picture etches forever on the soul one of the most terrible truths of life. It is this: whenever men go beyond their own humanity in committing their crimes, whenever they become so debased that they let themselves be possessed by a force of evil greater than human nature itself could conjure up, then human sin becomes inhuman, men are the offspring of beasts, and judgment lashes the soul with its most unspeakable terrors.

The Sixth Trumpet and the Plagues of Evil (9:12-21)

This scene is a variation of the preceding. Men have become so linked with the demonic powers of evil that John can see "the four angels who are bound at the great river Euphrates" (vs. 14). They remind us of the four angels who had to hold back the four winds of the earth until God's servants had been sealed (7:1-3).

Now the angels are released and the judgment which they bring is once more from the spirit world of evil. Frightful figures dash to war, fighters with flaming breastplates, on horses that have lions' heads and from whose very mouths fire belches forth (vss. 16-19). Again the judgment is partial (vs. 15), its goal being to bring men to repentance; yet men brazenly refuse all opportunity to turn back to God (vss. 20-21). And the writer, with a keen eye to the basic wrong in human nature, pictures the sin to which men cling so tenaciously as idolatry. Perhaps for him this consisted in emperor worship, but whatever its form in that or any other age, the worship of any but God is always the acme of evil.

The whole idea of men's being linked with the powers of the Devil may easily be laughed out of court; in fact, the Devil himself is but a figure of speech to most moderns. Yet John is focusing attention here on something real. Again his philosophy of life is sound. It simply is a fact that human nature can go beyond any human bounds in its descent to vulgarity. It is next to impossible to think of man as being able to conjure up all his inhumanities. Even as men must be possessed of the Spirit of God before they can ever rise to their own best selves, so it would seem that only when men are joined with the very demons of hell can they be as wicked as men have often come to be. And though God so arranges life that association with the Devil brings his character and judgment on men in time for them to see where they are headed and repent if they will, yet the pull of idolatry, the worship of that which is low, is so great that men often cannot let go their unholy union.

Interlude of the Bitter Scroll and the Two Witnesses (10:1—11:14)

First Part: The Message of the Scroll (10:1-11)

As there occurred between the sixth and seventh seals in the first cycle an interlude (ch. 7), so here between the sixth and seventh trumpets there appears a new interlude (10:1—11:14). And as in the former case the interlude was in two parts, the sealing of the redeemed of Israel and the sealing of the great multitude that no man could number, so this one also is in two parts, only much longer. It consists of the message of the scroll and the testimony of the two witnesses. The purpose of the interlude in each of the

cycles of seven seems to be largely dramatic. With the passing of
the sixth of the series we hold our breath in anticipation of the
end. But this dramatic writer does not allow the end to come with
such precipitation. He deliberately keeps us in suspense. Each
time he makes us wait to see the seventh of the series.

Such a procedure is, however, more than a literary device. It
is true to life. Oftentimes when it looks as though God's judgments
must surely be spent and the cup of men's iniquity be full, there is
a prolonged period in which the condition as it is seems to remain
unchanged awaiting some final decision. And in that waiting there
is opportunity to look around and gain fresh understanding of
what has been going on and especially what redeeming factors
God has introduced which men, in their hurried and often frantic
way of life, have not observed.

The first part of this present interlude is closely dependent on
Ezekiel's early visions. Most of it is really a rewriting and length-
ening of Ezekiel 2:8—3:3, a brief passage which ought to be read
with this chapter. But the additions to the picture in Ezekiel are
as noteworthy as the likenesses. Here the vision is of judgment
and mercy combined, as they so often are in the dealings of the
Lord with men. The judgment is portrayed in the "mighty angel
. . . wrapped in a cloud" (vs. 1). The cloud is always one of the
symbols of judgment. This impression is augmented by the terrible figure of the face of the angel looking "like the sun, and his
legs like pillars of fire." But the interwoven mercy is there in the
form of the rainbow of promise arched above the angel's head.

Heaven's complete mastery over the regions in which men live
is set forth in the stance of the angel, with one foot on the sea and
the other on the land (vs. 2), as a sort of divine Colossus of
Rhodes. "Sea" and "land" in apocalyptic literature denote the
source and seat of two kinds of evil among men, the sea suggesting the treachery of human government and the land the falsity
of human religion. So even here John probably means to say that
heaven has sway over the "little systems" of men, whether they
be political or religious.

One of the more curious devices of the Book of Revelation is
brought to bear at this point (vss. 3-4). Not only is any avid
anticipation of what the seventh trumpet will proclaim checked
by this long interlude, but another entire cycle of seven is thrown
on the screen momentarily and then removed after only a glance
has been permitted. The effect is tantalizing. This cycle of the

"seven thunders" was clearly witnessed by the writer—as clearly as the cycles of the seals and the trumpets—and he was "about to write" what he had seen when he was bidden to "seal up" what he had heard the seven thunders utter. Whether this is again a device used only for effect or whether it has some deeper significance is hard to say. Since John, like Paul, was a mystic, it may be that the message of the seven thunders was the one part of his complete vision which was too personal for him to lay before the eyes of others. Paul had been "caught up to the third heaven" where he had "heard things that cannot be told" (II Cor. 12:1-4). Serious-minded men may occasionally have such ecstatic experiences but they do not parade them before others. They speak rather of things that may be interpreted for the general good. What the seven thunders uttered John never tells; presumably their message had to do with the power of God in the earth. They may even have been suggested by the vivid description in Psalm 29 of the "voice of the Lord," a phrase which occurs seven times to declare in high poetry that "the God of glory thunders" (Ps. 29:3).

The angel, deliberately slow in arrival and of awe-inspiring presence, has been sent to declare that "there should be no more delay" (vs. 6). This pledge he makes most authentic by a fourfold vow (vss. 5-6), since his promise is for the world. He swears "by him who lives for ever and ever," then by him "who created heaven and what is in it," next by him who created "the earth and what is in it," and finally by the creator of "the sea and what is in it." The solemn pledge of God's sure action is, of course, measured in heavenly terms, not earthly; that is, the "delay" that is to be no longer may still seem like long delay to men, but it is not so in the annals of God. Similarly, the angel who appeared to Daniel near the end of his apocalyptic vision swore solemnly with uplifted hand that the delay in the fulfillment of Daniel's vision should be only for "a time, two times, and half a time," this three and a half symbolizing, as it so often does in an apocalypse, the short, cut-off time (Dan. 12:6-7). The assurance given John culminates in another reference to the impending seventh trumpet with the sounding of which "the mystery of God . . . should be fulfilled."

The solemn angel of this vision had in his hand "a little scroll" (vs. 2). This is not the same as the scroll of judgment which the Lamb alone had been found worthy to open (5:6-10). This scroll is already open, and it is John, not the angel, who is to make use of it. He is told to take it from the angel and "eat" it (vss. 8-9), even as Ezekiel had been bidden to do in the vision on which this is based. To "eat a scroll" of something written signifies to digest its message thoroughly. But whereas Ezekiel found only that the scroll which he ate was as sweet as honey in his mouth (Ezek. 3:3), John's experience is more profound. He shared with the prophet the discovery that the message was sweet as honey in his mouth, but he found that after he had eaten it, the taste was bitter in his stomach (vs. 10). Oftentimes a message of doom seems just what a prophet desires most to proclaim. It is "sweet in his mouth." He is all eagerness to tell of the righteousness of God and to show how far men fall short of it. But after he has had time to digest that message better, after his wider experience has led him to see what are the terrible consequences to men of the judgments of God, then, if he cares for men at all, he will be more and more loath to pronounce doom upon them; the very message of judgment will have become "bitter." But the man of God must keep on digesting and declaring God's Word whether it is palatable or not.

Second Part: The Two Witnesses (11:1-14)

As in the case of the cycle of the seals, it would hardly do to pass on to the terrors to be wrought by the seventh of this cycle without giving greater assurance than has yet been proclaimed. So John turns to the seat of worship, the Temple. We see first a measuring of the Temple, a figure which is often used in Scripture. The most elaborate measuring is recorded in the later visions of Ezekiel (Ezek. 40-42). Here Ezekiel, who was both prophet and priest, was led by an angel through each portion of the Temple which he anticipated in his dream would some day be built in Jerusalem. So also in others of the ancient prophets, the measuring of the Temple or of the city suggested rebuilding (Zech. 1:16; 2:1-5). Sometimes, as in Revelation, the measuring denotes a testing on the part of God to see whether the people are up to par. Thus Amos was told to measure the wall around the city with a plumb line (Amos 7:7-9).

This present vision, however, prepares the way for preservation. Those who worship in the Temple and at the altar are to be kept safe. If, as seems likely, the literal Temple in Jerusalem had been destroyed by the Romans (A.D. 70) before this book was written, it is still true to say that John was using the earthly Temple as the symbol of the Temple of God in heaven where those who measure up as true worshipers abide with him. These are probably thought of by John as the martyrs, those who have witnessed up to the point of death. The omission of "the court outside the temple" (vs. 2) is in keeping with the common notion that the Gentiles would desecrate it. "The nations," as they are called here—that is, those who were the pagans of society—would not respect this court of the Temple even though it had been provided especially for them. Jesus himself had declared that Jerusalem would be "trodden down by the Gentiles" (Luke 21:24). In Jesus' declaration no length of time is mentioned; it is simply a vague reference to the fulfilling of the times of these Gentiles or pagans. Here, however, John is sure that the desecration of God's holy place can last only "forty-two months," that is, three and a half years, which is the symbol of the cut-off, limited time, one half of seven. Similarly in Daniel the angel had declared that the time until "the end of these wonders" should be "for a time, two times, and half a time," that is, three and a half (Dan. 12:6-7).

All this is but prelude to the vision of the two witnesses (vs. 3) who are also "to prophesy" for "one thousand two hundred and sixty days," which again indicates three years and a half. That is, even while God's holiness is being desecrated by wicked human powers (in John's day probably Rome and the Roman emperors), God will not leave himself without witness in the earth. And just as in the old law the testimony of at least two witnesses was required to inflict the death penalty (Deut. 17:6), so God never leaves himself without sufficient witness to carry his judgments to their conclusion.

John's description of the two witnesses starts with a figure taken from the days of the Jews' return from captivity. The "two olive trees" were declared by the prophet to be "the two anointed who stand by the LORD of the whole earth" (Zech. 4:3, 14). In Zechariah's day these were presumably Joshua the new high priest and Zerubbabel the political leader of the Jews. The prophet thought of them as the human grounds for hope in his day, trees that were full of olive oil to light the lamps in the new Temple court. But John pays no attention to these persons of antiquity. After borrowing the figure he makes use of it as representing other and better-known "witnesses" for the Lord. The description that follows in verses 5 and 6 makes it clear that he is thinking back to the days of Moses and Elijah. In the memorable picture

of the plagues on Pharaoh in Egypt, Moses may be said to have
"poured fire" on the enemies of the Lord and to have caused their
death (Exod. 7-11). Likewise Elijah invoked on Mount Carmel
the God who answers by fire (I Kings 18:36-40). He also by his
powerful praying "shut the sky" so that no rain fell for three
years and a half (I Kings 17). Moses brought other plagues on
the Egyptians, including the turning of water into blood mentioned here (Exod. 7:14-24). No doubt these two historic figures
are used also because their names are joined in the expression of
hope at the very close of the Old Testament (Mal. 4:4-6), and
even more because of the fact that these two appeared before
Jesus and his inner circle of disciples on the Mount of Trans-
figuration (Matt. 17:1-8). Jesus himself had been mistaken for
Elijah (Mark 6:15). So John is on solid ground when he uses
Moses and Elijah as the two witnesses of God.

But the significance is deeper than any illustrations. Since two
witnesses were always required to authenticate truth, and the
word of one alone was not to be taken, John is saying again that
God never leaves himself without sufficient witness in the earth.
God raises up witnesses not only in the times of Moses and Elijah,
nor in the days of Jesus' ministry in the flesh, nor even in the
times of the Book of Revelation. Whenever men are needed to
bear testimony to the truth, they always appear at the right
time.

Moreover, such testifying personalities always give their lives
unto the death for God; they are the martyr type of witnesses
(vss. 7-10). John pictures their destruction at the hands of "the
beast that ascends from the bottomless pit," and he clearly lo-
cates the place of their martyrdom as Jerusalem where their Lord
himself had suffered. Describing the city allegorically as Sodom
and Egypt marks it as both debased and enemy territory. From
all parts of the earth, "from the peoples and tribes and tongues
and nations" (four sources once more), arises the merrymaking
with which callous minds celebrate too soon their apparent victory over the righteous. One can understand why the forces of
evil do thus rejoice at the temporary overthrow of witnesses to
God, especially when those witnesses are "prophets." For in their
heart of hearts they are afraid of the voice of the prophet who
fearlessly tells the truth; it is a "torment" to them. No wonder the
author represents the murder of the witnesses as accomplished
by "the beast that ascends from the bottomless pit." It is by his

demonic power that the faithful are put out of the way through the conniving of his crafty earth-bound followers.

True to his calling as an apocalyptist, John emphasizes the resurrection of God's slain witnesses (vss. 11-12). It is after the three and a half days, after the brief and limited time when witness-bearing seems to be stamped out, after men have had their little day of "freedom" from the tormenting straightforwardness of truthful men, that these witnesses share both in Christ's resurrection and in his ascension. "And in the sight of their foes they went up to heaven in a cloud," reminding us again of Elijah, who was carried to heaven in a whirlwind of final triumph (II Kings 2:9-12). Thunderstruck men gaze on the rising of the true witnesses to a new power. The revived witnesses become themselves judgmental. They are "in a cloud"; there is "a great earthquake, and a tenth of the city fell." The spiritual truth of this scene can never be far from the needy Christian. Just at those times when faithful witnesses seem to be gone from the Church, when all freedom to witness is apparently wiped out by some autocratic power, God takes such moments to bring his faithful testifiers back to life. Man's extremity really is God's opportunity.

The Seventh Trumpet: Announcement of the Impending End (11:15-19)

The full-voiced proclamation of the angel of the seventh trumpet is the triumph song for which the saints have been waiting, beginning in a slow, soft strain and rising gradually to full swell. The angel is not declaring something which takes place all at once; he is gazing into the future and predicting what the climax will be like when it does come. Not only will Christ set up his Kingdom; he had told his followers while he was with them in the flesh that "the kingdom of God is in the midst of you" (Luke 17:21). But that Kingdom is now to be made up of the very conquered "kingdom of the world." The result of such a marvelous announcement of God's victory in the earth is that the twenty-four elders of the vision in chapter 4 "worshiped God" (vs. 16). Their song which follows (vss. 17-18) stresses the beginning of God's reign in all the earth, the wrath of God as manifested at the overthrow of his foes, and the reward that comes to God's servants. The most secure note of all is sounded in the reopening of heaven and the sight of "the ark of his covenant" within God's

Temple (vs. 19). So the apocalyptist returns at long last to the point at which the prophet had begun: God's eternal Covenant with his children.

Now it would surely seem that the end of all things is upon us. But just as in the seven seals, so with the trumpets: the blowing of the seventh trumpet issues in another new cycle, perhaps the grandest and the most typical of all the book. The seven mystic signs that it presents are full of the imagery of conflict which characterizes the apocalyptist's message. The good and the evil are divided into two sharply contrasted forces, each led by mighty powers. The battle is on to the finish. If the Lord is to take his great power and reign, he must be able to lead to triumphant glory his loved ones who are sore beset.

THE CYCLE OF THE SEVEN MYSTIC SIGNS
Revelation 12:1—14:20

John, as a true apocalyptist, believes firmly that life's issue is determined in mighty conflict. His scheme of cycles has been built toward this end. At first glance it may seem that such a view of the Christian experience is contradictory to what we have in other parts of the New Testament. Does not Paul teach what we call the doctrine of "sanctification," according to which the man who is "in Christ" grows more and more in his likeness unto the perfect day? (See, for example, II Cor. 3:17-18; Col. 3:10.) And does not John in his Gospel assume a fellowship of oneness with Christ that has resulted from a new birth (John 3), so that it has become second nature for the child of God to be like him? Is not the Christian life one of steady, even though sometimes slow, growth toward that full-orbed glory which both Paul and John know as "eternal life"?

But the author of the apocalypse looks at life as an almost continual battle for spiritual existence. He sees the foes of the soul so strongly arrayed against the Christian that doom looks all too sure. And he views the triumphant ending of the Christian's story, not as the attainment of growth, but as the hard-won decision that lies beyond a tense and bitter bout. Moreover, he does not view the struggle as one which goes on unseen within the soul. To him it is placarded before heaven and earth, spread over all the billboards that line the arterial highways of life. Nor does he think of the strife as human; it is a superhuman struggle that goes on in every soul. God and the Devil are arrayed there against each other. Every would-be saint of God is battleground for the cosmic strife. The Devil contends for every man and gives way only after fierce contest. But God will not desert the soul in its agony. He sends his own Son, who died for man, to fight with the adversary on man's behalf. All the hosts of heaven and hell, angels and demons arrayed against each other, spar and stab in hand-to-hand conflict over one human soul. And John believes that for everyone who has responded to the call of Christ the victory is the Lord's.

After all, such a view of the Christian experience is not out of keeping with the major portion of our New Testament. Paul himself speaks of a war within himself and thinks of himself as "wretched" on its account until Christ delivers him (Rom. 7: 13-25). In all ages and by all leaders Christians have been warned not to think of themselves as being "carried to the skies on flowery beds of ease," but to recognize that they must sail "through bloody seas" as others have had to do before them.

Yet nowhere else besides the Book of Revelation do we find such clear and single picturing of the issues of life. Nor is there any other writing in which the lines are so pointedly drawn or the hosts so spectacularly arrayed. This book is the chief of all those that depict our Lord as contending unto the very end for the ones whom he has redeemed. But his victory is assured because, as the Lamb of chapter 5, he contends with the blood of his own sacrifice.

The present cycle, unlike those of the seals and the trumpets that have gone before, contains no numbering. Yet it is almost certain that the writer had in mind, consciously or unconsciously, some arrangement of the usual seven. So, without the aid of numbers, most scholars have read these central chapters of the book as a new cycle. Some indeed find two sets of seven in these scenes. We shall treat them all as one cycle, noting three great representations of evil pitted against three glorious figures of good in this fierce final fight, with the believing saints—the Church, we would call it—as the figure in between, over which the two sets of forces do battle. In picking out these all-important parts in the great drama, we must remember that angels are never thought of in the apocalypse as chief characters; theirs are always supporting roles. They draw out and amplify the conflict, but they are never the winning or losing contestants themselves. With this in mind we shall find that the seven "mystic signs," as we would call them, fall naturally into the usual groups of the three and the four; only the three come first this time, representing—not on earth but in heaven—the struggle that goes on for the souls of believers. The two spiritual forces, one good and the other evil, are in command.

The Direct Struggle: the First Three Signs (12:1-17)

First on the scene is the one over whom the strife is occasioned, "a woman clothed with the sun" (vs. 1). She has great power in herself, since she has "the moon under her feet," and she is crowned with a diadem of twelve stars, the number of the Church. She does indeed symbolize first the Jewish Church which was the mother of the Christ and then the Church of the Lord Jesus Christ over which the contest between God's grace and the hatred of the Evil One rages to the utmost.

The figure will probably seem somewhat mixed, yet it is not too difficult to follow. The woman bears a son, who is obviously the Christ, since he is referred to in the language of the Second Psalm as the one who is to rule the nations with a rod of iron (vs. 5). Moreover, the child is "caught up to God and to his throne," a reminiscence of Christ's ascension to the right hand of power, which plays so impressive a part in this entire drama. That Christ should be at once the child of the Church and the redeemer of the Church is good to contemplate, and his twofold role here—on the one hand helpless until he is snatched up to heaven, on the other hand glorious in might when he is by his Father's throne—is a picture thoroughly consistent with the dual presentation of throne and Lamb in chapters 4 and 5. This time there are no figures in the Old Testament to suggest such a scene. Many have called attention to the fact that we do find in Greek myths stories of heavenly women with sons, but there is really no antecedent for the spiritual message found here.

Opposite the woman and her child, still viewed from the vantage point of heaven, stands the "great red dragon" (vs. 3), with his seven heads denoting great wisdom and his ten horns, mighty power. The seven diadems upon his heads, and the sweeping of the stars of heaven with his tail, is indeed a terrifying portraiture of evil might that seems destined to overthrow the very throne of God himself. Apparently John means to suggest that the dragon knows where the real danger to his kingdom lies, for he "stood before the woman . . . that he might devour her child when she brought it forth" (vs. 4). If only he can capture and destroy the Christ himself at the outset, he will make easy work of the woman and all her other offspring, perhaps even of God himself. We are reminded of how serious an assault the Devil made on Jesus immediately following his ordination to his public ministry at his baptism, tempting him three times to bow down to the power of evil and to own that Satan was the real prince of the world (Matt. 4:1-11). We shudder too before an even deeper scene—Satan's attempt to conquer Jesus when he was faced with the immediate prospect of the Cross, and the agony of struggle in Gethsemane when the Master met and overcame his last and greatest temptation (Luke 22:39-46). While the great red dragon of John's vision had seven heads, he must have lacked complete wisdom; for had he but known it, when he lost the fight with Christ himself, he lost it forever, since it is well said of Christ, "because he himself has suffered and been tempted, he is able to help those who are tempted" (Heb. 2:18).

When the Christ is caught up to heaven the mother is left without any immediate protection. So John sees her fleeing to the wilderness where God has prepared a hiding place for her for "one thousand two hundred and sixty days"—again the three and a half years of the short, limited time (vs. 6).

Meanwhile the dragon, who is the Devil, in John's wondrous vision carries the warfare right through the gates of heaven. He is determined to conquer the Christ. The remainder of chapter 12 (vss. 7-17) describes this heavenly warfare, first from the standpoint of what goes on in heaven itself, and then with a foreboding look at what is to transpire on earth when the Devil is finally cast down to it. All the angels of heaven, led by Michael the archangel (vs. 7), are called into the fray and they cast down the Devil and his angels. Then it is that the hymn of the anticipation of Christ's glory with the Father is sung (vs. 10)—"the salvation and the power and the kingdom of our God and the authority of his Christ." We are not surprised at the assertion that the implementing cause of the celestial victory was no mighty human armor, but "the blood of the Lamb" and the "word of their testimony" (vs. 11). Here again is the emphasis on the life that has been totally given up for God, and again the recurrent stress on the martyr as the real witness. The shout of joy for the deliverance of heaven from the dragon's attempted conquest is mingled with the warning to the earth of his embittered wrath (vs. 12).

There is almost the mock heroic about verses 13-17. Having lost the main center of the battle, the Devil belatedly remembers to go after the woman whom he had allowed to escape into the wilderness. Apocalyptic symbolism stops at nothing, and it does not hesitate to represent that the woman-church fled his advances with the aid of two great eagle wings, denoting the double power of spiritual flight, and even with the temporary assistance of the earth itself. Her suffering at her tormentor's hands is again to be for only "a time, and times, and half a time," once more the three and a half that is just half the complete number seven and therefore incomplete and limited. Perhaps the most gigantesque figure in this paragraph is that of the dragon, now called "the serpent," pouring out water like a flood after the woman-church while the flood is gulped up by the earth as fast as it comes!

The real glory of the passage lies in the fact that heaven is made secure against all evil—secure by sacrifice. But there is a breathtaking glimpse of a different kind of struggle yet to come. This is seen in the experience of the tormented woman in the wilderness. It is also found in the terrifying remark that the dragon, overcome with fury at his inability to drown out the Church, "went off to make war on the rest of her offspring, on those who keep the commandments of God and bear testimony to Jesus" (vs. 17). While this is, from the Devil's standpoint, a less vital contest, he can be expected to throw into it the most subtle of his onslaughts just because he has been thwarted heretofore. The Devil, having lost the fight to seduce the Christ or overcome him, keeps up on earth through the years his repeated efforts to capture the children of the Church. We who are among those children have experienced his most wicked wiles!

The Indirect Struggle: the Next Three Signs
(13:1—14:5)

The Fourth Sign: The Beast from the Sea (13:1-10)

There is no surprise so stupefying as an indirect attack. When one is looking for the coming of some evil with which he is familiar, he feels himself at least partly prepared. But when that evil seizes him, not in the shape he knows and expects to combat, but in some unforeseeable form, then truly he is at a loss how to proceed. The surprise which chapter 13 holds is that the Devil, the great red dragon, does not attack the rest of the offspring of the woman-church directly. But he employs the roundabout way of delegating his power to another! And delegated power is harder to fight than any direct attack just because it is so difficult to recognize.

The creature to which the dragon gives his authority is described as "a beast rising out of the sea" (vs. 1). As we have seen, the sea in apocalyptic literature is the usual symbol for human government, and John looked on this human government as evil. The New Testament writers do not always take this attitude. In spite of the fact that the early Christians generally faced authority that seemed to them hostile to the authority of Christ, they often bowed to it as rightful in its own sphere, and they even praised it. Thus Jesus himself bade his disciples pay their half-shekel poll tax even though he insisted that the sons of the Kingdom were free, for he was determined that he would not needlessly "give offense" (Matt. 17:24-27). He also uttered his famous "Render to Caesar the things that are Caesar's" when he was confronted with the Roman coin, though he was quite insistent at the same time that it was of supreme importance to render "to God the things that are God's" (Mark 12:13-17). Paul exhorted Christians in the capital of the empire to be grateful as well as obedient in their political relations, recognizing that even a pagan government was "instituted by God" to resist wrong and support good (Rom. 13:1-7).

But by the time of the writing of the apocalypse, Christians had suffered so much at the hands of the empire that they could no longer contemplate any good restraining force that it might have had. When a government sets itself to order religious worship, then its paganism stands out beyond any other quality. When it attempts to dictate what men may believe and what deity they may honor, it is no longer the institution of God but the very tool of the Devil. Like the sea, it divides one people from another; it can be thought of only as a "beast" coming up out of the sea.

For John that government was, of course, Rome. True enough, it had at one time been very liberal toward all religions. But John was facing the way in which the later Roman emperors had come to persecute the Christians and to separate family from family, friend from friend, pastor from people. From the religious viewpoint of John, the Roman government had become devilish in its actions. So he describes this sea-beast as resembling the dragon very closely. Like him it has "ten horns and seven heads," only in this case the diadems are on its horns of power instead of on its heads (vs. 1). That the seven heads may have been suggested by major emperors of Rome would have been appropriate enough, and that the ten horns suggest some ten lesser rulers in the empire is quite likely, even though we may be unable to determine with any consensus of opinion just who they were. But the significance lies once more in the number scheme itself. John is saying that this monstrous human government is vicious power, completely crowned—ten diadems on ten horns—and he is saying it in cryptographic fashion so that his Christian readers may understand him and the officials of the Roman government never guess what he is talking about. The "blasphemous name upon its heads" is evidently that of self-worship, honoring the emperor as god. Such a beast can be likened only to a leopard and a bear in its stealth and to a lion in its roaring (vs. 2). These figures are, of course, reminders of Daniel's beasts (Daniel 7). But the significance of this creature far exceeds that of any similar symbolism of an older day. For the dragon gives "his power and his throne and great authority" to this beast from the sea. The fact that his gifts are three in number indicates that the writer thinks of this false government as a spiritual evil and therefore more terrible than if it had been only human.

Since the satanic power of the universe can no longer be directed against the Christ himself, it is focused on the Church of believing Christians. And one of the surest ways to beleaguer Christ's followers is to raise up over them a government that is autocratic, one that seeks to compel them either to adopt a certain form of religion or else to put the government ahead of whatever religion they may embrace. And this is far easier to accomplish than men realize. Almost unconsciously they think of their first allegiance as being to their state. Even if they are devout Christians they tend to put the flag of country above the cross of Christ. Not only in a kind of government that is atheistic, but much more subtly in one which has the outward trappings of goodness, men are deceived. It is not that such governments are necessarily totally evil. Caesar and Hitler alike built fine roads and brought some much appreciated gifts to the lives of the common people. But it is that these governments, and all other man-made powers, tend to usurp the place which, for the Christian, can be held by the Kingdom of God only. It is that any human government, however good, may lose the position it should hold as God's restraining force and may come instead to require for itself an allegiance that belongs to none but Christ. When this happens, as happen it does over and over again, then the true Christian can only assert the priority of his conscientious faith in God even if it means that he, too, must join the long line of the martyrs. For any Christian, loyalty to the Kingdom of heaven takes precedence over loyalty to his nation.

But it is not alone in literal governments of the earth that this truth is manifest. Wherever in human society one group or one individual lords it over others, there the name of God is blas-phemed. Where one culture or race or economic level takes ad-vantage of its position to force another to comply with its will, there the name of God as well as the name of humanity is taken in vain. Wherever a mother seeks to determine whom her chil-dren shall marry or where they shall live, wherever a father in-sists that his son follow the vocation he has planned for him, wherever an individual becomes a political boss or a financial tyrant or a dictator of any sort, there the Devil has once more delegated his authority to the sea-beast: government, however good it may appear, has too much power; it has become a beast.

John's use of current events in order to express his theology branches out at this point to include a legend. He says that one of the heads of the sea beast "seemed to have a mortal wound, but its mortal wound was healed" (vs. 3). In the latter part of the first century there was a frightening tale making the rounds that Nero, who was supposed to have committed suicide in his insanity, had really gone into hiding and was coming back again at some critical moment to avenge himself on his adversaries. As the years went by and he did not appear, the legend changed in form to suggest that someone else would rise in Nero's spirit to be a more terrible dictator still. The coming of Domitian to power in the 80's and 90's seemed, for many Christians as well as others, to fulfill this terrible expectation. It is probable that John makes use in the present passage of this legend of "the returning Nero" or "Nero Redivivus," as it was often called, to state his belief that though evil seemed to be put out of the way in the state when Nero received his "mortal wound," it came back in the

new Nero in even stronger force. Whether we are right in thus
interpreting John's use of the background of the first century, the
theology he bases upon it is again fearfully true. Evil does have
a reviving power that often looks greater than the revival power
of the Church or than even the resurrection of Christ. It gets
many a "mortal wound," but the wound is often "healed." No
wonder "men worshiped the dragon" who had given his power to
the beast, and said sadly of the beast, "Who can fight against it?"
(vs. 4).

The activities of the beast are as wide as the universe (vss.
5-10). It blasphemes God and his heavenly dwelling (vs. 6) and
conquers all the saints (vs. 7). It extends its authority in all
worldly directions, again represented by the four of "every tribe
and people and tongue and nation." As is usual with the apocalyptist, John believes that those who escape have been determined beforehand; they are those whose names have been
"written before the foundation of the world in the book of life"
(vs. 8). Even the price they will have to pay is determined, for
some are "to be taken captive," yet just as surely is it prede-
termined that anyone who slays them will himself be slain with
the sword (vs. 10). John uses for this assurance a direct quota-
tion from one of Judah's greatest prophets who also believed in
God's overruling authority (Jer. 15:2). And for such an un-
changeable fate he has the key words, "endurance and faith."

The Fifth Sign: The Beast from the Earth (13:11-18)

In the "dramatis personae" of this great stage presentation John
brings on the inevitable beast from the earth to serve the interests
of the beast from the sea. His function is to get men to "make
an image for the beast which was wounded by the sword and yet
lived" (vs. 14) and to "worship the image of the beast" (vs. 15).
His is obviously, then, a priestly power; he represents false religion. With his "two horns" he even looks "like a lamb," the
great central figure of the Christian religion itself (vs. 11). The
take-off on the crude religious deceptions of John's day is not
hard to follow. Roman state cults not only made images of emperors for men to worship, but were "allowed to give breath to
the image of the beast so that the image of the beast should even
speak" (vs. 15). The schemes by which priests of that day pulled
wires behind the temple images so that their eyes seemed to glow
and their mouths to move would seem to us laughable if it had

not been such a serious matter. The superstitious of all ages have been easy dupes of priestcraft. But still more importantly, this beast of false religion backs the requirement that every man must be marked with the mark of the beast which is false government, and must lose all rights to trade or even buy food unless he is so marked (vss. 16-17).

Again John's theology overleaps any background of his own age. It is always true that the worst possible combination that evil can concoct in this world is the union of bad human statecraft with bad human religion. The support of false government by false religion that looks innocent—"like a lamb"—is the most devilish achievement of the underworld. And again this happens, not at any one time, but over and over again in the history of the world. One may well think, as he reads these verses, of the support often given to tyranny by the Roman Catholic Church, as in Spain or in South American lands today. One bows his head in shame as he remembers the countless times when the Protestant Church has stood behind the state as it compelled the labor of little children or of slaves. It is not that John is here "predicting" the Roman Church or any of our own, but that he is asserting a philosophy of history which comes to pass whenever or wherever false religion and false government get together.

It should be noted how pointedly John pictures the powers of evil imitating the forces of the Kingdom of God. Not only does the sea-beast have a wound from which he dies, coming back to life in mimicry of the resurrection of our Lord, but here we have the unholy trinity of the dragon and the sea-beast and the earth-beast—the Devil and his delegated powers of the wicked state and the wicked religion—as a bizarre aping of the holy Trinity of the Christian faith. Evil always has a demoniacal ability to "look like a lamb"; that is the reason it captures so many. Once more, it is because the head of the forces of evil retires from the scene himself and works through his delegated creatures that he is almost able to deceive "the elect" (Matt. 24:24).

Yet John is confident that even this kind of power will fall short. The sea-beast exercises his "authority" for only "forty-two months," again the three and a half years of the limited time (vs. 5). And as the inspired seer comes to the close of this ugly part of his vision his eyes are opened to the fact that such a power is known by its "number," and that number is never a series of sevens, which would represent the complete power of

God, but always a series of sixes—"six hundred and sixty-six,"
which, as John points out, is "a human number" (vs. 18). The
most devilish power of all, working through men, always falls just
short of perfect authority.

In John's day there can be little doubt that the number 666
found its appropriateness in the working out of a human name.
In every alphabet each letter has a numerical value, so that one
may work out the "number" of any name. If the name of the
emperor is expressed in the Greek form, "Neron Caesar," and
then rewritten in Hebrew letters, with the values which they
have in the Hebrew alphabet, the result is exactly 666. It is perhaps significant that if we take the more familiar Latin form,
"Nero Caesar," the result is 616, and this number actually occurs at this point in some of the Greek manuscripts of our New
Testament. But this assurance that John had in mind the frightful
Nero, whom many of his readers could remember and whose return they feared, must again not cause us to limit this saying to
Nero or the first century. Nor must it make of us adepts in spell-
ing out the numbers of other names to see how many we can
find down through the course of history that have actually
equalled 666. Protestants have sometimes eagerly grasped at the
fact that the names of some of the worst popes can be so spelled
out. Some Romanists have as mockingly discovered that they can
work out the name of Martin Luther to make the same fateful
number. But this is not the point. The deep truth is that wherever
men set out "conquering and to conquer," as in the case of the
rider on the white horse (6:2), wherever devilish purpose is
cloaked under the guise of selfish human government pretending
to rule for the good of men and supported by a religion (whether
of state authority or not) which slavishly bids its devotees follow
the will of the government—whenever such a combination of
forces is at work, there the achievements are terrible but they
still fall short of their goal. They are sixes and not sevens, and
for this all true Christians who suffer for their faith may thank
God and take courage.

The Sixth Sign: The Lamb on Mount Zion (14:1-5)

The first three of the mystic signs represented the ultimate
struggle as going on in heaven: the war between the dragon and
the son of the woman, fought over the woman herself. The remaining four of these signs directly affect men on earth. Two of

them have been evil, the sea-beast and the earth-beast. The remaining two are good. And just as the first two are actually the Devil in other forms, so these two are the ascended Christ in varied likenesses, the first of which is the Lamb.

The Lamb on Mount Zion is a welcome intervener in the sly evil that has been going on. And he does not stand alone; with him are the "hundred and forty-four thousand" that have his name (vs. 1). That he should come to Mount Zion is natural; Micah had prophesied, "Out of Zion shall go forth the law" (Micah 4:2). That he should be accompanied by a multitude of the faithful, and that this multitude should be described as the square of the church number, twelve, multiplied by the cube of the round number ten, is simply the apocalyptist's way of saying that the full number of the redeemed are with Christ. They remind us of the 144,000 who were sealed (7:3-8). The new song which they sing to the accompaniment of harps (vss. 2-3) is obviously the song of redemption. Yet, with all the freedom of thought and movement which the writer of apocalypse always assumes, he pictures the redeemed song, even though given on Mount Zion, as sung "before the throne and before the four living creatures and before the elders" (vs. 3). These are readily recognized as figures of the great scene of worship in heaven (ch. 4) whose symbolism dominates all the remainder of this book. The preciousness of the song of redemption is emphasized by the fact that none may know it except the redeemed themselves (vs. 3).

The redeemed are symbolized by chaste and spotless souls (vss. 4-5). In the original they are called "virgins." From this it has sometimes been assumed that John places virginity on a higher plane than married life. This does not necessarily follow. Virginity, because it implies chastity, is taken as a suggestion of purity in the same way that debauchery is taken as a sign of impurity. Moral purity is the symbol of singlehearted loyalty to Christ. What the writer is saying is that in the midst of all the chicanery of this wicked world, where false rule and authority are supported by false worship and where the very arts of the Devil seem always triumphant, Christ can still stand with followers who are not only tried and true but pure in heart. Verily, John's faith did not lag!

Interlude of Angelic Messengers and the Blessed Dead
(14:6-13)

First Part: The Message of the Three Angels (14:6-12)

Once more, as we draw near the end of a particular cycle, we anticipate some glorious scene. That Christ should stand on Mount Zion with the complete group of his spotless followers, even when the world is filled with iniquity, would naturally suggest this. But instead, as in the numbered cycles, we are held up by an interlude between the sixth and seventh, and, as before, that interlude is in two parts.

The first portion bids us listen while we wait. And as we listen we hear first an angel proclaiming a blended message of the "eternal gospel" and the "judgment" of God (vss. 6-7). Once more, this message is sounded abroad to all parts of the earth, symbolized by the four: "every nation and tribe and tongue and people." Even the judgment of God is here associated with his "glory," for judgment is the activity of God's holiness.

The song of the second angel is in a minor key; it proclaims with great solemnity the fall of "Babylon" (vs. 8). That Babylon was John's secret name for Rome seems evident. The literal Babylon of the Old Testament had always stood for a pagan power that was rich and profligate and proud and that was doomed to destruction (Dan. 4:30-31; Jer. 51:7-8). Almost these very words are used of the impending fall of Babylon in the prophetic literature (Isa. 21:9). Metaphorically, Rome was Babylon come to life again—yet come to life only to fall under God's judgments as ancient Babylon had fallen.

The third angel proclaims (vss. 9-12) with "loud voice" and in direful figures the fate of those who worship the beast (that is, the sea-beast) and the image of it which the earth-beast set up and bade men hallow. He is the angel of an eternal torment, pictured in terms of the pouring of unmixed wine to represent the undiluted wrath of God (vs. 10). That this torment is to be "in the presence of the holy angels and in the presence of the Lamb" is in keeping with many other scenes of this book where the deepest sting that bitter conscience is dealt is that it must suffer while utter purity is looking on. Nor does the writer think in terms of a purgatory from which ultimate release may come; this is a torment from which the smoke "goes up for ever and ever" (vs. 11).

No wonder this curious interlude of the call of the three angels is closed with a new warning that the saints of God need endurance to face such scenes (vs. 12).

Second Part: The Blessed Dead (14:13)

The other part of the interlude is lovely in spirit. "Blessed are the dead who die in the Lord . . . for their deeds follow them!" Cynics have never believed this. Even Christians are sometimes tempted to feel that life is wasted, that the good does not last. But here the assurance (which is always strongest at the point of the interludes) is given that to die "in the Lord" is not only to "rest from their labors" but to know to a certainty that all that has been done in the name of the Lord will be established by him.

The Seventh Sign: The Reaper on the Cloud (14:14-20)

The climax of the mystic signs is reached with another picture of the victorious Christ, this time as a reaper with his sickle, gathering in the vintage of God's wrath in final judgment. That he himself is judge is symbolized by the fact that he is seen seated on a white cloud (vs. 14). The call of an angel bidding him reap is followed by words that remind us of the interpretation of Jesus' parable of the Weeds of the Field (Matt. 13:36-43). The accompanying angels who reap with him heighten the scene. Comparing the judgment to a wine press which is trodden out (vss. 18-20) recalls the similar use of this figure in the prophet's portrayal of God's wrath (Isa. 63:1-6). That it was trodden "outside the city" probably means outside Jerusalem, a suggestion of retribution for those who compelled Jesus to die outside the city. That blood flowed from the wine press for sixteen hundred stadia (two hundred miles!) apparently suggests that it covers the whole earth, since 1600 is the square of the earth number four multiplied by the square of the round number ten.

In the mystic signs, then, we have had the high theology that the issue of all life is determined by a spiritual conflict, a heavenly combat which affects the earth. It is the faith of the writer that in such a conflict the eternal power of God and of his sacrificed Christ are arrayed against all the hosts of hell. God sends his Son with blood, the blood of sacrifice that purifies and saves. He gathers his own to his side while he is coming in judgment on all the evil. To live in such a faith is to appreciate the fact that all the

struggle which goes on in the earth is but the reproduction of the
spiritual conflict between heaven and hell. It is to believe that life,
in its last analysis, is "a fight to the finish," but that the One who
is for us is greater than all that are against us.

THE CYCLE OF THE SEVEN BOWLS
Revelation 15:1—16:21

Having presented judgment in the form of a great drama, the
author is now ready to bring upon the scene a cycle which depicts
judgment as complete. This is done in terms of great bowls filled
with the wrath of God (15:7). The appropriateness of such a figure lies in its suggestion of huge containers of unmixed wine, a
picture that is employed more than once in Scripture to represent
the undiluted fury of God's anger against sin. But before the cycle
actually is thrown on the screen there is an elaborate preparation
just as there was in the case of the cycle of the seals (ch. 5) and
that of the trumpets (8:1-5).

Preparation for the Pouring of the Bowls (15:1-8)

This cycle resembles those of the seals and the trumpets, but it
differs from them in one particular. While they pictured partial
judgment that affected only a third or a fourth of this growth or
that, the new judgment is final and complete (vs. 1). The little
chapter of preparation, however, deals with what is always the
chief concern of this writer—the safety of those who believe in
Christ. In the present case that safety is made vivid by another
mention of the sea of glass which is found in the great scene of
worship in heaven (4:6), only in this case that sea "mingled with
fire" (vs. 2) suggests the heavenly replica of the Red Sea which
the saved of Israel crossed in their escape from Pharaoh. That
theirs is now a spiritual state is emphasized in their threefold victory, for they have "conquered the beast and its image and the
number of its name." The song that they sing to the accompaniment of their harps as they stand by the glassy sea is appropriately
called "the song of Moses . . . and the song of the Lamb" (vs. 3),
for Moses had led the Israelites across the literal Red Sea into
the Promised Land, and the Lamb leads the martyred saints to
their final crossing of the stream of death into life. The song itself

(vss. 3-4) is the worship of God whose just judgments have been revealed. It is ccmposed in the Hebrew rhythm and with typical Hebrew structuie of lines in alternating parallelism; that is, the first line and the third carry essentially the same thought, as do the second and the fourth, and so on.

Following this hymn of the redeemed there is an awesome opening of "the tent of witness in heaven" (vs. 5). This scene, too, is evidently suggested by the experience of Moses, as he prepared to enter the presence of God when he had completed the erection of the Tabernacle (Exod. 40:34-35). While in the Hebrew text of Exodus the Tabernacle is called "the tent of meeting," in the Septuagint, or Greek, translation of this passage it is called by these very words that John uses, "the tent of witness." The significance for John lies, of course, once more in the root meaning of the word "witness," the word from which we get our English "martyr," the word that describes those whose faithful witness has taken them even to death for their Lord. The glory of God that filled the heavenly tent with smoke is again the reminder of that glory which so filled the first tent of meeting with smoke that Moses could not enter it. The majestic appearance of the seven angels as they appear with the seven last plagues is indicative of the fact that we are nearing the culmination of this drama. Their pure linen and their golden girdles at their breasts (vs. 6) are emblematic of their priestly function in worship; yet they are the bearers of the full measure of God's wrath on the unrepentant earth.

The First Six Bowls (16:1-12)

The figures in this cycle of the bowls are largely repetitions of those that occurred in the cycles of the seals and the trumpets and are based again on the plagues of Egypt. Once more, the first four affect directly the human sphere (vss. 2-9). The first bowl is poured on the earth (vs. 2), the symbol, as we have seen, of false religion; and appropriately enough it afflicts with fearful sores those "who bore the mark of the beast and worshiped its image," that is, those of the great drama in chapters 12-14 who were taught by the earth-beast to worship the image of the state-beast (13:12). The second bowl is poured out into the sea (vs. 3), the seat of false authority in government, and total destruction of life takes place. The third bowl is poured upon "the fountains of

water" (vs. 4), symbolizing the sources of truth, and the bloody-
ing of the waters that follows occasions a direful duet between the
angel of the water and the altar concerning the justice of the
wrath of God (vss. 5-7). Taken out of its setting, this song might
suggest only human vindictiveness, but in this connection it be-
tokens the fact, everywhere acknowledged in Scripture, that God
has the right to bring to eternal judgment all the evil machina-
tions of man. Especially is this true when those evils are what they
are here—the attempt of men to prostitute human government to
the ruin of their fellows. This song is but the fulfillment of the
eternal truth attributed to the deliverer Moses who declared of
God in his farewell address to Israel, "Vengeance is mine" (Deut.
32:35), a prediction expanded by a late New Testament writer to
include God's judgment on all the people (Heb. 10:30). The
fourth bowl is poured on the sun, but the result is not the sun's
disappearance from heaven; rather, it is a scorching of men with
such torrid heat that "they cursed" (or, more exactly, "they blas-
phemed") God instead of repenting to give him glory (vss. 8-9).

As in the case of the earlier cycles, the fifth, sixth, and seventh
of the present series transport us to the spirit world. With the
pouring of the fifth bowl, the kingdom of the sea-beast is devas-
tated (vss. 10-11). The sixth bowl is emptied "on the great river
Euphrates" (vs. 12), so as to dry it up and thus better prepare
the way for those mystic figures known as "the kings from the
east" who will sweep over the land (vs. 12). While this suggests
as background a feared Parthian invasion of the empire of John's
day, it is essentially a scene of the spirit world where one evil
force is used by God to destroy another.

Interlude of the Frogs and the Battle of Armageddon (16:13-16)

It is perhaps not mere fancy to see once more, before the
seventh of this cycle, an interlude, and again one that is in two
parts. The first part is the vision of the "three foul spirits like
frogs" (vs. 13) that issue in turn from the three figures of the
evil trinity which were described in detail in chapters 12-14.
These figures are here called the dragon and the beast and the
false prophet, putting in somewhat clearer terms the Devil and
the sea-beast and the earth-beast, the last being a prophet of a
false religion. That these mighty powers which assayed to con-

quer the earth, and which in their might and glory seemed to be unbeatable, should finally produce from their mouths, as from some green slimy pond, nothing more than three froglike spirits is a devastating caricature of the failure of evil. That which men fear most because it appears to be mighty and eternally entrenched becomes at long last only a ridiculous spawning of sickly creatures of the night. That these are "demonic spirits, performing signs" (vs. 14) makes them not the less susceptible to the blasts of "God the Almighty" on his "great day."

And what is that great day? The writer calls it, in the second part of his interlude, the day of "Armageddon" (vs. 16). For some reason this word has had a strange fascination for literalists in their use of the Bible. Perhaps its history accounts in part for this. "Armageddon" is a transliteration of the Hebrew words "Har Megiddo," meaning "Mountain of Megiddo." There was no literal mountain of this name, but the reference is probably to the mountains that were near the town of Megiddo, or possibly to the large size of the mound of the city itself. This place stood at the upper entrance to the Plain of Esdraelon, Israel's chief battleground of antiquity. From here the Israelites had witnessed the spectacular overthrow of the apparently unbeatable forces of Sisera, when "from heaven fought the stars" on the side of the people of God (Judges 5:19-20). Into this Plain of Esdraelon by Megiddo the Syrians, and later the Assyrians, must have traveled when they besieged Samaria (II Kings 6, 17). By this route Alexander the Great had proceeded when he undertook to find in the Orient more worlds to conquer. All down through history this region has been known as a bloody battleground and as a convenient pass for great armies. In a word, "Megiddo" had come to stand, in Jewish and therefore in Christian thought, for great and decisive struggle. John uses it here only, and he does not have in mind any thought that at some particular date in time the forces of evil and the powers of good will literally fight it out at this spot. It rather stands for the great final overthrow of spiritual evil by the spiritual power of the Almighty God.

The Seventh Bowl: Destruction in the Air (16:17-21)

After this significant interlude which almost breathlessly anticipates the end, the seventh angel pours his bowl into the air (vss. 17-21). When the air is destroyed, all life is gone; the judgments of God are complete. In keeping with this finale a great voice from the Temple proclaims, "It is done!" (vs. 17). One is reminded of Jesus' words from his triumphant cross, "It is finished" (John 19:30). The completion of judgment and of salvation go hand in hand. The writer clings to his use of apocalyptic symbols in picturing the scene, four great demonstrations in nature heralding the final effect on earth (vs. 18), which for John can be put in no more terrifying language than that there fall on men gigantic rocks of hail, each "heavy as a hundredweight" (vs. 21). The complete destruction of the earth is symbolized in the passing of every island of the sea and every mountain (vs. 20). The vision of the destruction of life itself which is about to be worked out in detail is previewed in terms of the falling of the great city "Babylon" (vs. 19). With such a vision ends the last of the numbered cycles, the outpouring of the complete judgment of God's wrath.

THE CYCLE OF THE EPISODES OF FINAL JUDGMENT
Revelation 17:1—20:15

The Book of Revelation is supremely concerned with the judgments of God. That these have to do both with the destruction of evil and with the salvation of those who put their trust in God broadens the idea of judgment beyond that which we usually give to it. But it is typical of the Bible to deal with judgment by this larger outlook. Thus all the cycles in this book interweave the doom of evil with the saving of the good. From chapter 6 through chapter 11 these judgments have been only partial in nature: destruction has fallen on only a part of the earth and of human life, and the martyred dead receive only part of their reward, being told to rest until their number is complete. But from chapter 12 on, the picturing of judgment has been of that which is final. In chapters 12 through 14 this has been accomplished, as it were, upon a stage, human life being thought of as a struggle to the end between good and evil persons in the world of spirit. In chapters 15 and 16 final judgment has appeared as a numbered cycle, the wrath of God poured out as unmixed wine from the huge bowls of his celestial banquet hall. Now, once more we have a picturing of final judgment—this time the grandest and mightiest spectacle of all. We can best describe these scenes as *episodes* of judgment. And once more we shall probably not be untrue to John's thought if we see in them an arrangement of seven. The figures will prove still more daring than any that have gone before; the outcome of the episodes will prove decisive and final.

First Episode: The Harlot City and the Beast (17:1-18)

When the last sketch is to be made of utter evil, what form should it take? We have had the representation of beasts, and that returns with this new portrait. But we have here two other figures, not so frequently used in apocalyptic literature, but perhaps more precise and meaningful still. This cycle of episodes begins by painting evil as a loathsome woman and as an animalistic city. If we recoil from such ideas, we can look ahead and note that John, ever a lover of contrasts, intends to conclude his story of salvation by picturing righteousness as a lovely woman, the bride of the Lamb (19:6-8), and as a beautiful new city let down out of heaven on the earth (21:1—22:5). John conceives of womanhood as capable of the lowest dregs of degradation and also of the most refined loveliness that can be imagined. He thinks of the city as the congestion and rotten dump heap of all that is morally putrid in life, but he thinks of it also as symbolic of the presence and the glory of God.

In the current scene the harlot woman is "seated upon many waters" (vs. 1). This would apply literally to the suggestive name that is given her, "Babylon the great" (vs. 5), for Babylon was located upon many streams. But it is obvious that this name is but a thin disguise for Rome, and that all John's Christian readers will understand that he is calling that city a cesspool of evil and a woman of shame. Though Rome did not actually sit on many waters, it was near the sea, and the designation can roughly apply.

It is significant that in order to get the perspective of what this wicked city is actually like, John does not try to view her from within; rather he is carried away "in the Spirit into a wilderness" (vs. 3). His view becomes objective; it is taught him by a higher interpreter than he could find within the city gates. From such a vantage point he comes to understand that the city is a den of vice, and he daringly pictures her as drunk, not with the wine of man's making, but with the beastly mixtures of her own vicious career (vs. 2, and again at vs. 4). This mixture later turns out to be the blood of saints and martyrs (vs. 6). By that swift change of figure so common in this book, John then beholds the woman, no longer symbolizing a city herself, but riding a beast that stands for the wicked city (vs. 3). Like the sea-beast of the dramatic struggle (13:1-4), this replica has "seven heads and ten horns." But while we would be prepared to understand that these are symbols of perfect sagacity and complete power, John seeks to work out in greater detail their import in the history of Rome.

The description of this beast sounds very confusing and we may not be able to follow with sure-footedness all the way the writer would take us in his lurid painting of the Rome of the first century, but his general idea can hardly be missed. He apparently thinks of the beast as the city over which wicked emperors have reigned and are reigning. They would have to be seven in number to fit in with his apocalyptic symbols and they would have to be emperors who assumed not only authority but rights that went beyond those John felt were intended for human beings. Just which emperors he meant to include in his group we cannot be sure, but we may feel certain that the list would contain such names as Augustus, Vespasian, and Titus, who destroyed the Temple at Jerusalem, as well, of course, as the abominable Nero. John thinks of himself as living in the days of the sixth of the seven blasphemous rulers, the last one being destined to fall in "a little while" (vs. 10). That the beast "was, and is not, and is to ascend from the bottomless pit and go to perdition" (vs. 8) is augmented by the fact that "it is an eighth but it belongs to the seven" (vs. 11). Bizarre as this sounds, it is once more the picture of the legend of Nero who had died but was to come back and meet a still worse destruction—a legend that John first worked out in the sea-beast with the mortal wound that was healed (13:3). Again we have in symbolic form the doctrine that evil, however complete and powerful its appearance, and however great its ability for revival, will surely fall; it reigns but "one hour" (vs. 12). Overtones of the struggle of chapters 12-14 return as the forces of evil support the beast and make war on the Lamb (vss. 13-14). All peoples of the earth, represented by the four sources, "peoples and multitudes and nations and tongues" (vs. 15), are included in the vast assemblage. The "ten horns" (vs. 16) are probably rulers of lesser rank than emperors. But this time the Lamb not only conquers, he is given his final title, "Lord of lords and King of kings" (vs. 14).

Such is the nature of the final concentration of evil; it is like a beast, like a harlot, like a rotten city. We are ready now to behold in detail its judgment.

Second Episode: Judgment of the Harlot City (18:1-24)

Much of the language used to paint the story of "Babylon's" fall is poetic in structure; the song of doom is recurrent. An angel (vs. 1), then "another voice" (vs. 4), then the "kings of the earth" (vs. 9), most especially the "merchants of the earth" (vss. 11, 15) and "all whose trade is on the sea" (vs. 17), and then finally another "mighty angel" (vs. 21) take up in turn the lamentation. This chapter is not hard to understand but it is all too easy to evade. The emphasis on evil's strangle hold in the economic world mounts as the dirge increases in intensity. The description of the foulness of the city's economic life (vss. 1-3) is followed by a new emphasis on her pride (vss. 5-7), and these occasion the certainty of her impending downfall (vs. 8) and the need of God's people to separate themselves from her life (vs. 4). The keen satire on the merchants who are so chagrined at her doom and yet who stand at a safe distance from it (vs. 15) is surpassed only by the brilliant enumeration of their articles of trade which culminates in "human souls" (vss. 11-13). The repeated wails of those who have lost all their wealth in the downfall of the city that they thought to be impregnable (vss. 14-19) is followed by a single shout of joy from heaven (vs. 20). The pride of Babylon-Rome recalls the pride of ancient Babylon which the prophet stigmatized (Isa. 47:8-11). The groans and taunts of those who have lost all in her destruction bring back to mind the hissing of the maritime merchants of former days when Tyre fell (Ezek. 27:32-36). The final dirge of the "mighty angel" (vss. 21-24) is altogether in the minor key. It reminds us of the prophet's declaration that ancient Babylon would fall with a mighty thud into the sea (Jer. 51:59-64). All the joy and the profit in this later Babylon's life have been felled in one awful hour because she had garnered her riches while shedding "the blood of prophets and of saints" (vs. 24).

Thus these first two of the final episodes (chs. 17 and 18) go together in portraying this unique picture of the nature and the judgment of evil. That the lust for economic gain lies at the root of all the harlot's impurity and gross sin is appropriate both to the figures used and to the reality of life. Rome's single monetary system and economy throughout the earth had made this truth particularly notable in John's day. It was inevitable then that the merchants should have close control of the government. But it is true in any age that greed for gain, for economic supremacy, lies behind the cruel predatory drives of national and international economic groups, supported, as they so generally are, by the military state. The pleading note that God's people may see and "come out of" such an order before it is too late is the apocalyptist's way of joining the prophets in urging on Christ's followers an altogether different sort of life.

Third Episode: The Hallelujah Chorus (19:1-5)

We like to think of a Hallelujah chorus in the style of Handel, where the Hallelujah is the triumphant worship of the reigning Lord. And John comes eventually to such a chorus. But he is realistic enough to know that first there must be the equally triumphant rejoicing over the downfall of evil at the hand of God. And so in this vision we get "the mighty voice of a great multitude in heaven" (vs. 1) shouting to God their threefold paeans of praise, "Salvation and glory and power," because of his just and complete judgment on the harlot-city. Again the scene is reminiscent of the throne of God in chapter 4 from which all these visions have issued; and other figures of that scene, the twenty-four elders and the four living creatures, join the refrain (vs. 4). It is touching that the final note of praise in this mighty chorus is reserved for all who are "his servants . . . small and great" (vs. 5).

Fourth Episode: The Marriage Supper of the Lamb (19:6-10)

The Hallelujah chorus turns now to a worship of God Almighty, a worship sung with "the sound of many waters" (vs. 6), a saying that reminds us of the sound of the voice of the Son of Man as he stood in the midst of his Church (1:15). And it is to this very Son of Man that the attention of the heavenly audience is directed. For the victorious Lamb, there is now prepared the celebration of his wedding day on high. The experienced Bible reader will be accustomed to this figure of God taking his people as his bride. Thus the Old Testament had anticipated the union of the Lord with his redeemed in such passages as Isaiah 54:5-6 and Hosea 2:19-20. Jesus himself had compared the coming of his Kingdom to a wedding feast for which the guests must be ready (Matt. 25:1-13). Paul had thought of himself as preparing the people of his churches to be the bride of Christ (II Cor. 11:2).

As in any human wedding, the attention is focused on the bride more than on the bridegroom, and on her dress more than all else. John not only accepts this habit of human nature but uses it to fine advantage in describing the costume of the heavenly bride (vss. 7-8). It is of "fine linen, bright and pure" in contrast to the gaudy garments of purple and scarlet and gold that were worn by the harlot (17:4). But more significant is the saying that the fine linen of the bridal gown "is the righteous deeds of the saints" (vs. 8). Protestants sometimes hesitate to talk about good deeds for fear of being lured into belief in the doctrine of salvation by works which characterizes much of Roman Catholic thought. But while our good deeds do not justify us, and we depend entirely on the grace of God for our redemption, there is still judgment to face, and that judgment is in accord with our doings. Salvation does not occur in a vacuum nor does it end in enjoyment of a privilege. We are saved to a purpose, and that purpose includes the creation within us of Godlike character and readiness for service. It includes, in John's language, "righteous deeds." To think of such deeds as the material from which is fashioned the wedding gown of the Lamb's bride is indeed a daring figure but one that is consistent with John's other symbols.

The Lamb's bride is, of course, the Church. It is the Church that is made up especially of those who have given their lives wholly to God's Christ, those who are represented in this book by the martyrs. To say that the good deeds of the Church make the garment she wears on her day of final betrothal to Christ is in effect to lay the responsibility on each member of the Church. John compares the privilege of the ones who have thus participated in the preparation to the blessedness of those who are fortunate enough to be invited to the great "marriage supper of the Lamb" (vs. 9). To be left out of the list of invitations to a wedding is a sting most people have felt at one time or another. To be invited to a gala marriage is an honor worth waiting for. So it is that John anticipates this greatest honor of all.

There are two surprises in this wedding picture. One is a warn-

ing against the worship of an angel (vs. 10). Moderns hardly
need that caution, but to the ancients the temptation to angel
worship was real. Paul warned one of his churches against it
(Col. 2:18). That the angel of this vision could represent himself
as simply one of John's brethren who was a "fellow servant" with
him in the worship of God was a drastic pattern of thought for
this writer to employ. For us it has the practical value of reminding us that no creature, however grand in appearance, is
worthy of our veneration save God alone.

The other surprise is the unique statement of the theme of the
heavenly vision, "For the testimony of Jesus is the spirit of
prophecy" (vs. 10). Here John, as the greatest of all apoca-
lyptists, joins hands with all the prophets to proclaim that Jesus'
testimony to God—his complete revelation of God—is the very
spirit and heart of the entire message of God's Word. If there is
a "Golden Text" to the Book of Revelation, this is it.

Fifth Episode: The White Horseman (19:11-16)

The married Christ now appears on the white steed of his
victory. We noted at the first appearance of a white horseman
(6:2) that the figure of a rider on a white horse does not itself
tell whether his mission is beneficent or deadly. White is the
symbol of victory in this literature, and both the tyrant and the
benefactor may display it. Decision as to which kind of character
he may be waits on further description of his nature and purpose
and on the outcome of his riding. In the sixth chapter, the white
horseman was bent on conquest and he was followed by warriors
that represented strife and famine and death. In this instance, the
white horseman "is called Faithful and True" (vs. 11). His warfare is not selfish conquest, as all human warfare is, but is done
"in righteousness." The eternal Christ is the only one who *can*
wage a righteous war. This, of course, is again not a picture of
some one particular event at some special point of time. It is the
symbol of essentially the same triumph that we saw in the reaper
on the clouds (14:14-20). Moreover, his appearance is pictured
in terms that have become familiar in earlier scenes. His eyes of
fire and his sharp sword have been sketched before, in the initial
vision of the Son of Man (1:12-16). His armies are the armies
of truth, clad in the same pure white linen that the Lamb's bride
wears (vs. 14). This conquest, then, is righteous and this judg-

ment is just. Although he has a secret name that none may know (vs. 12), the name that he reveals is the complete title his followers would rejoice to hear: "King of kings and Lord of lords" (vs. 16). Unmistakably he is the Christ, "The Word of God" (vs. 13).

Sixth Episode: The Destruction of the Beast and the Prophet (19:17-21)

As we draw near the end of these final episodes of God's universal judgment the conquering Lord makes ready to destroy altogether those that have been his great adversaries. In dramatic fashion "an angel standing in the sun" (vs. 17) bids the vultures of the sky to gather to a great feast where they may gorge themselves on the flesh of the mighty (vs. 18). This carrion meal is obviously the contrast to the wedding supper of the Lamb, and it is the setting for the capture of the sea-beast and the prophet— the earth-beast that had worked wonders in his sight (ch. 13). Thus does John envision the final overthrow of all human government and of all human religion that supports it. That he can see them "thrown alive into the lake of fire that burns with brimstone" (vs. 20) is the recognition that their gross deceitfulness receives its just reward. That the sword with which the Lord and King slays their followers "issues from his mouth" (vs. 21) is a final vindication of the initial picture John had drawn of the Son of Man (1:16) and of the fact that this white horseman had, among his other names, that of "The Word of God" (vs. 13).

In a sense this episode also presents something which occurs often in history. In each age the Christ rides victoriously to overthrow the power of false religion and false government that have conspired to wreck that age. But in a deeper sense we have come now into the portion of the book where John is describing finalities for all ages and all time. There shall come a day when the human dictatorship shall reach its last sea, and that shall be, not a sea of its victory, but a lake of fire (complete defeat and judgment) into which the Lord himself drives these dastardly foes of his Kingdom. Then indeed he can take his throne and reign!

While Christ comes back again in many senses—comes to the individual believer at his death, to the Church at its time of crisis, to each age to bring it to judgment—it is also true that in a very real way there is a final "coming" of the Lord. Judg-

ment, though it goes on from day to day, is brought to bear at
last in complete form upon all humanity and upon the very satanic source of evil. Judgment and salvation are alike both present and future, and the White Horseman brings both to completion in his coming to reign.

Interlude of the Millennium, with the Binding and Loosing of Satan (20:1-10)

The inspired author has brought us up to the very brink of
that which is final. The sea-beast and the earth-beast—or the
beast and the false prophet, as he has come to know them—have
been cast into "the lake of fire that burns with brimstone" (19:
20). All evil is now conquered and put out of the way except
the Devil himself. Since there is one more of the seven episodes
yet to be enacted, we should expect it to deal with the destruction of the Devil and the final enthronement of God as the eternal
victor, and we should look for this to happen at once. But with the
finesse of the artist, as well as the truthfulness and understanding
of the saint, John pictures the climactic finish as delayed once
more. The seventh episode, that of the great white throne, does
not appear until the very last paragraph of chapter 20 (vss.
11-15), and in the meantime we behold the strangest of all the
interludes, that known as the millennium, a word which means a
thousand years. Once more it is in two parts, the binding of
Satan (vss. 1-6) and the loosing and final destruction of Satan
(vss. 7-10).

The particular items which this short passage includes are not
hard to enumerate, though some of the more important of them
have often been overlooked. The seer beholds an angel coming
down from heaven armed with the key to the bottomless pit and
with a great chain (vs. 1). He reminds us of the fallen star, symbolizing a fallen personality, whom the fifth of the angels of the
trumpets introduced and to whom the key of the abyss was en-
trusted (9:1). To the angel of this present figure is given the
authority, not to bring to an end the career of the Devil, but to
bind him for a thousand years (vs. 2). It is important to note
that it is an angel, and not the Christ, who effects this binding.
When the Devil is thrown into the "pit" and covered over so that
he cannot get out, the great relief that humanity enjoys for this
thousand years is that he cannot "deceive" them any more. John

identifies Satan with the serpent in the Garden of Eden, who proved himself "more subtle than any other wild creature that the LORD God had made" (Gen. 3:1). It is never the direct frontal attack of the Devil on men which they need fear the most, but always the sly, underhanded ways by which he gains his ground. A thousand years of freedom from such beguiling seems to the writer to be truly a calm rest period when mankind may take a deep new breath of life!

But the millennium is not simply negative; it is not alone the absence of the dragon's direful trickery. It is a time for the proclamation of victors. Again it is vital to note who it is that lives and reigns during this thousand years—not everybody who has been saved, but only the martyrs (vs. 4). They are pictured as being raised up and as seated on thrones, not only because they "had not worshiped the beast" but chiefly because they "had been beheaded for their testimony to Jesus." Once more the apocalyptist throws stress on the lives that have been given up for God. He carefully distinguishes them from all others, going so far as to say that none of the rest of the dead are raised to life in this millennial blessedness. But he uses one of the beatitudes of this book to pronounce special benediction on the martyrs who thus share in what he calls "the first resurrection," and he looks forward to their greatest reward as deliverance from "the second death" (vs. 6). Moreover, they are not to reign alone, but they are to hold their thrones along with the reigning Christ their Lord (vss. 4, 6).

But the author, though he paints this scene in glorious colors, does not think of it as lasting beyond the "thousand years." It does not suggest an eternal blessedness, nor does it usher in the complete overthrow of Satan. For after the thousand years have passed, the Devil is to be loosed again from his prison (John does not attempt to say how!), and he then will be free to continue his old tricks—he "will come out to deceive the nations" (vs. 8). John seems here to envision the most widespread deception of all, for the Devil is to go through all the earth and gather the most powerful of all the armies of evil from "the four corners of the earth," an army with which he surrounds even "the beloved city" (vss. 8-9).

This recuperative power of the Devil, so like the revival of the sea-beast's head that had been wounded and was healed (13:3) or like the beast that "was, and is not, and is to ascend from the bottomless pit" (17:8), is ever a favorite theme with John. We have pointed out before how true it is to life. When evil appears to be bound in unbreakable chains, marvelously it gets unshackled. But John pictures the Devil, though escaped from captivity for a terrifying thrust, eventually overthrown with all the more terrific force and hurled into the lake of fire and brimstone forever to join his agents, the beast and the false prophet, who had already been destroyed (vs. 10).

Interpretations of the Millennium

Such is the restatement of the picture of the millennium. That it has caused a perfect welter of differences of interpretation in the Church throughout the ages, and that it has received attention far beyond the importance suggested by its meager length, is one of the strangest facts of biblical usage. The whole idea of a millennium rests entirely on this one passage; the figure occurs nowhere else in Scripture. There are a few portions of apocalypses outside the Bible that faintly resemble this section; the nearest thing to it in Scripture itself is the idea of evil angels chained for a time "in the nether gloom until the judgment of the great day" (Jude 6). The thought of a thousand years is used elsewhere in the Bible only to suggest that such a time, so long in men's experience, can be like a single day to God (Ps. 90:4; II Peter 3:8).

Interpretations of the meaning and significance of these few verses have ranged far and wide and have occasioned several divisions in the Church, as well as the formation of numerous sects. Most of them thrive on some interpretation of the passage that is more or less literal. The vagaries of the most extreme of them would not be of particular importance to us if they had not caused such a deep rift in the Body of Christ. They have given rise to types of theology that have often led the Church to injure both its evangelistic and its educational service to mankind.

Among the interpretations that have been largely literal, the *premillennial* and the *postmillennial* are the two best known and most influential. Both of them teach a millennium that will come in the course of time and at a definite period of history, though sometimes this is thought of as a literal period of a thousand years and sometimes the round number one thousand is considered to be approximate. However, their great point of difference from each other lies in their thought of Christ's relation to the millennium. According to the "premillennialists," Christ is to return to the earth before the millennium comes about, as the "pre" in the word suggests; in fact, it is he and he alone who can usher in the period of millennial blessedness and freedom from the Devil's wiles. According to the "postmillennialists," on the other hand, Christ is to come to the earth after the millennium has paved the way for him, as the "post" indicates; he caps the final climax to the period of bliss by making eternal the triumph over Satan as a postlude to his being held in chains for the thousand years.

Now at first glance it would seem to matter very little which of these interpretations one adopted, if he were to see in either of them the truth John was symbolizing. Both of them look for a blessed period of time in which the earth will be relieved of Satan's tormenting attacks, whether Christ comes in person before or after that time. But they have given rise to types of theology that are quite widely separated, and which have tended to develop quite different expectations concerning the Church.

The Premillennial View

Premillennialism has insisted that the period of bliss, and therefore the freedom from Satan's corrupting influence, cannot come upon the world until Christ returns in person. It generally proceeds from there to argue that Christ will not come until the world gets so far corrupted from the Devil's actions that it can no longer go on. Often this interpretation insists also that the Church itself is being more and more invaded by the spirit of Satan and is getting worse and worse. Premillennialists frequently call attention to the fact that the last of the seven churches in chapters 2 and 3 is the worst—Laodicea, the lukewarm church (3:14-22). And since many of them believe that the vision of the seven churches is a picture of seven consecutive ages of time, they formulate rather readily a system in which the Church goes more and more downhill until it must be "spewed out" of the Lord's mouth. In fact, premillennialism is logically a religion of pessimism so far as the Church is concerned, and while not all premillennialists follow its logic all the way, many of them are satisfied with the belief that both world and Church are getting worse and worse, since this state of affairs should hasten the return of Christ to usher in the millennium. There is, of course, always plenty of evil in the world and plenty of hypocrisy in the Church that may be pointed to as evidence.

If one is to take literally the figures John uses, the premillennialists have a strong point. The figure on the white horse who comes upon the earth (19:11) does precede the millennium and he is unquestionably the Christ. No one can deny the fact that he is present when the millennial reign is ushered in. Moreover, during the thousand years of blessed relief Satan is only bound, not destroyed, and after this another period, the length of which is not suggested, comes to be. But the difficulties of this interpretation are greater than its advantages. For if the Christ comes to the world before a definite period in which the Devil is bound, he ought himself to be able to dispense with the Devil, not just chain him. Moreover, in John's account, Christ does not himself even bind Satan; it is the angel who binds him (vss. 1-2). Christ seems to accomplish little by coming before the millennium, for the time of blessedness is all too short and the Devil soon gets free again to go up and down the earth and torment the nations worse than ever. If Christ has come and has not been chased out again by the Devil's release from the pit, why can he not do something about this revival of evil? Of what use is the great anticipation of his return if it results only in a short period of bliss followed by more hell on earth than there has ever been before?

Moreover, in the preaching and teaching of premillennialism there is often to be found but little emphasis on the work of the Holy Spirit. This is logical, since the Church is usually thought of as becoming more and more apostate under the influence of the world. It is the sudden and dramatic return of Christ that is to set things at rights. The sanctifying work of the Holy Spirit is not denied in premillennialism, but the Spirit is thought of generally as being able to save only a few brands from the burning. More and more attention is given to Christ's coming again in the flesh to deal with sin and bring judgment and salvation, though it is difficult to see why this is necessary, since "Christ, having been offered once to bear the sins of many, will appear a second time, not to deal with sin but to save those who are eagerly waiting for him" (Heb. 9:28). Since he dealt with sin by coming in the flesh, one would suppose that he would bring final salvation by coming in the spirit.

There is, however, a good side to the history of premillennialism. It has captured the urgency of Christian living. It has been strong in its emphasis on Christ's command to "watch" (Mark 13:37). Though it has laid far too great an emphasis on the out·

wardly spectacular, and has dealt with the signs of Christ's coming as though they were physically visible portents at some one
moment in time, and though it has often endeavored to figure out
a date when that coming could be expected, it has at least kept
churchmen on their toes. If it has sometimes produced a morality
that is the product of fear, it has generally made men conscious
of their need for personal reformation. Where it has fallen short
on the moral side of life has been in its frequent failure to come
to grips with social evils. This, too, has sprung logically from its
position, for if Christ is coming again in the flesh and coming
soon, it does not matter overmuch that men live in poor housing
conditions or that racial injustice is practiced or that wars recur
in rapid succession. Indeed, as we have noted before in another
connection, all these things may be in themselves signs of "the
end" and of the coming of Christ to usher in the millennium.

The Postmillennial View

Postmillennialism, on the other hand, is under the necessity of
finding some explanation for the picture of the coming of Christ
before the twentieth chapter (19:11). Since it, as well as premillennialism, generally interprets his return in the flesh literally,
it must resort to the thought that Christ's coming is simply *pre-
dicted* in chapter 19 and that he does not actually appear until
the revelation of the great white throne (20:11). This is a rather
violent handling of the text of the book. It has often been skipped
over by proponents of this point of view, but one can hardly get
away from the fact that if he interprets Revelation literally in
sequence, Christ comes before the millennium.

The advantages of postmillennialism lie in its theology. It can
preach with conviction the work of the Holy Spirit, for it is he
who strives with the Church against the world and prepares the
Church for the return of Christ. And while this does not have the
immediate dramatic effect of making men conscious of something
about to happen, so as to keep them urgent and expectant, it does
draw attention to the many quiet and effective ways in which the
Spirit of God is striving with men all the time. Moreover, the
postmillennialist does not view Christ's return as ineffective, for
it is at his coming, after the period of millennial bliss, that he
throws the Devil into the lake of fire and ushers in the judgment
and salvation of the great white throne (20:10-15).

Still, the notes of literalism remain in either of these interpretations of the millennium, leaving them not essentially different from each other. One result has been that many have become what is popularly known as *a-millennialists*, that is, not believing in the millennium at all, but thinking that John has mistakenly introduced into this figurative writing a lapse into some more or less literal view of temporary bliss.

But why take his picture of the millennium literally? If the other parts of the book are figurative, why should not this be? And though it is true that both premillennialists and postmillennialists frequently take portions of this scene in a figurative way, especially the period of the thousand years, yet they (and the a-millennialists too) always think of it as *some* period of *time*. But time itself is one of the apocalyptic symbols, portraying a truth that is real. A thousand years need not be any space of time at all, but only the idea of something good that is rounded out, as the cube of ten suggests.

An Apocalyptic Interpretation

Starting from this point, then, we may outline another interpretation of this passage in keeping with the earlier portions of this commentary. For want of a better name we shall call it the *apocalyptic* interpretation. To formulate such an explanation is important, for surely John intended the millennium to be taken seriously since he gave it this important location in the interlude of his last great cycle. We cannot dismiss it as easily as the a-millennialists who do not believe in a millennium at all.

An apocalyptic interpretation of the millennium would go something like this. It is a beautiful and true thought set down between the final overthrow of the Devil's emissaries, the beast and the false prophet (19:20), and the final destruction of the Devil himself (20:10). It has to do, not primarily with Christ or his coming, but with the power of the lives of the martyred saints (vs. 4). These saints are part of the court of judgment. They are the ones, and the only ones, who come to life again and are raised up to reign with Christ in the thousand years of millennial bliss. John distinctly says, "The rest of the dead did not come to life again until the thousand years were ended" (vs. 5). He calls this "the first resurrection" and he anticipates that those who share it will not need to fear "the second death" (vss. 5-6), which is evidently separation from God. He calls them God's "priests," and they reign with Christ for the thousand years. It is they who have

been introduced along with the angel who came down to bind the
Devil for the thousand years, and it is impossible to escape the
impression that these saints are the cause of the angel's being able
to bind Satan so securely.

Now when we remember that in apocalyptic literature, and
especially in this Book of Revelation, the role of the martyrs is
most important, and when we recall that the martyred dead really
stand for all those who give their lives completely to Christ, this
picture begins to take shape. God's angel is able to "bind"—that
is, to restrain—Satan and all his power wherever there are those
who have not counted their lives precious to themselves. He binds
Satan for a thousand years, that is, not for any length of time, but
with a perfect and complete binding, symbolized by this cube of
ten. Or, to put it another way, those who give their lives completely to Christ just as completely bind the power of the Devil.

This interpretation does justice to John's way of using symbols.
It also does justice to his Lord's strong emphasis on the Cross.
Jesus insisted that anyone who really came after him would have
to take up his own cross daily and follow him (Luke 9:23). And
such a cross does not mean a burden to be borne, it means a death
to be died. It is not important that that death be a literal, fleshly
experience. The believer must daily die to sin; he must daily die
to self; he must daily endure the suffering unto death—in business, in politics, in the home, even in the Church—which comes
to those who follow the way of Christ, resisting any form of
paganism which others would force upon them.

The fact that John and the Early Church thought of this cross-
bearing as proceeding all the way to actual death indicates that
such a result was very common in their time. It is increasingly
common in certain parts of the world in our own time. And both
because it was common then and because actual martyrdom is
the simplest way to think of taking the cross of Christ, the figure
suitably expresses the completely yielded life. But in any age, and
in any part of the world, wherever one dares to take seriously the
Kingdom way of living, he will suffer for it. It is not that if the
worst comes to the worst he may have to go to the cross, but that
in our pagan environment, to take Christ seriously is to ensure
the fact that there will have to be some sort of death of the self.
Possessions, ambition, independence, even life on this earth, may
be the price of complete loyalty. Physical martyrdom is the fitting
symbol of all other kinds of martyrdom. To die for Christ, quite

literally, may not be actually harder than to live conscientiously for him, but death is the natural figure to employ for all such surrendered living.

The Surrendered Life and Millennial Power

Such a use of the symbol causes the idea of the millennium to glow with meaning. Wherever Christ's servants give their lives entirely to him, wherever they die for him, whether literally or in the life of each day, there the angel of the Lord binds the power of Satan. There it is that those who thus give their lives to Christ are "raised up" into a newness of life, the "first resurrection," where they experience the bliss of being victors with their Lord. Both those who have suffered physical martyrdom for him and those who "die daily" for his sake know the meaning of triumphant living as no other can. In their lives, and as far as their lives extend, the Devil is completely bound, bound a "thousand years," ten times ten times ten, the most perfect binding that John can express by his figures.

What then of the "loosing of Satan," according to such an interpretation? "When the thousand years are ended" (vs. 7) would simply mean the condition outside the lives and influence of the martyred saints. Beyond the sphere of their utterly surrendered lives, the Devil is free to roam at will and "deceive the nations." There is no other power on earth that can bind or restrain him save the power of the given life. He can even wax bolder and gather more forces of torture wherever there are no lives that are Christ's very own. That gathering of forces is pictured (vs. 8) in terms of Ezekiel's war with "Gog, of the land of Magog" (Ezek. 38:2; compare 39:6). To try to identify these figures with any known kingdom, either of Ezekiel's day or of John's or of ours, is to miss the point of the use of the figure. If, as some suppose, the land of the Scythians suggested this terminology to the writer, he uses that only as a symbol for all the worst enemies of the people of God. The identification one sometimes hears today of Gog and Magog with white and yellow Russia has no standing in fact whatever. These are figures of speech to John, appropriate because a prophet of God's ancient people had used them. In employing them John is putting his approval on the belief that wherever there is no one willing to sacrifice his very life for Christ, the Devil is not only freed from his chains, but can gather up all the refuse of humanity and the spiritual powers of evil in his last vile attempt to overthrow the Kingdom of Christ. And "their number is like the sand of the sea" (vs. 8).

It should be noted that this blessed reigning with Christ has its limitations. It takes complete giving of life to experience complete blessedness, represented by the perfectly cubical figure of the thousand. Moreover, even when lives are completely given, all they can do is to *bind* Satan; they cannot destroy him. The most beautiful Christian life in all the world is not enough to put the Devil finally out of the way. Only God in Christ can do that. It is heavenly fire that comes down to *destroy* the Devil and his hosts with final and complete overthrow; it is only from heaven that the power can come to cast the Devil himself into the lake of fire and brimstone (vss. 9-10).

It is possible that it may seem to some that John is unchristian here, or that he simply has confused with his Christian faith some pagan notion of revenge. For he pictures the Devil and the beast and the false prophet, not as being annihilated, but as being "tormented day and night for ever and ever" (vs. 10). But this is consistent with the remainder of the New Testament, and especially with the words of Jesus. Our Lord did not anticipate any purgatory in the next world, where evil would be gradually purified and delivered, but he spoke in terms of a hell of everlasting anguish "where their worm does not die, and the fire is not quenched" (Mark 9:48). If such an eternal punishment is envisioned for ordinary men who are unrepentant, how much more for the Prince of Evil who turns them against repentance? It is true that God is "not wishing that any should perish, but that all should reach repentance" (II Peter 3:9). Universal salvation would be true if God's will were responded to by all. But men will not allow universalism to be true. The Devil himself is pictured here and elsewhere as being stubborn to the end. And stubborn rebellion against God is so terrible that it can but drive both demons and men away from his presence. Once driven away from God, completely by their own willfulness, they cannot repent—not because God is unwilling, but because in the very nature of the case they have set themselves stonily against the only One who could work salvation in them.

Belief in the millennium, then, ought to be held on to, not indeed as a weird anticipation of some time in history when there will be a temporary letup in evil before the final consummation, but as the symbol of the great restraining power that God has given to men, a restraining power which can bind even the father of wickedness if it will go the full way of the cross, but a restraining power which can never finally destroy evil itself. For such magnificent power bestowed on the followers of Christ we may be deeply grateful, and for its greater manifestation in the earth we well may ardently pray.

Seventh Episode: The Great White Throne (20:11-15)

The last one of the last of the cycles most appropriately centers where the visions of the cycles first issued—in the throne of God. He who sat on the throne is pictured as so utterly powerful, so dominant in rule, that "from his presence earth and sky fled away, and no place was found for them" (vs. 11). It is the victorious throne, for it is white. This is first of all the throne of judgment, before which all the dead, "great and small," are judged (vs. 12). Once more apocalyptic literature stresses the fact that no man is privileged in the sight of God. Man is man, and all men are treated alike. But there is not only the opening of the books of judgment before this wondrous white throne of God; "another book was opened, which is the book of life" (vs. 12). Here is the idea we have met with before in Revelation, the same stress on deeds as the basis of judgment which Jesus made in his parable of the Great Assize (Matt. 25:31-46). The judgment of "Death and Hades," or death and the grave, is the final touch of doom. That anyone whose name is not discovered in the "book of life" is thrown into the lake of fire is but a reminder that the destruction of evil is for the purpose of the redemption of the good. Righteousness could not live forever in a condition of torment from evil. The separation of the sheep from the goats in Jesus' parable, as the division between the evil and the redeemed here, is in order that God's glorious salvation may appear in all its worth.

THE NEW HEAVEN AND THE NEW EARTH
Revelation 21:1—22:5

Like the quiet beauty of a sunset after a day of storm, this lovely scene of the new heaven and the new earth follows the long struggle portrayed in the Book of Revelation. But as in such a sunset the splendid colors are generally to be seen climbing over the clouds that still remain, so in John's picture there are glimpses of the angry blackness against which this new radiant light appears all the more glorious.

There is much in the Old Testament to suggest the symbols that are used here. The early chapters of Genesis contribute a goodly portion, for we have here the virtual remaking of the Garden of Eden. Prophetic pictures from the Books of Isaiah and Ezekiel find large representation, for their authors envisioned mighty transformations. It is also at this point that the Book of Revelation resembles most often the Gospel of John, with its stress on such figures as the light and the water of life, and on such teachings as the worship of God without need of temple. Yet with all his evident use of these biblical backgrounds, together with his possible dependence on the suggestiveness of Babylonian and other myths, the author of Revelation at no point shows more clearly his gift for making the figures and thoughts of others over into something new and rich. He is distinctively the inspired Christian revealing the vision which God has given in a very special way to him.

God's New Dwelling-Place (21:1-4)

That John should see "a new heaven and a new earth" (vs. 1) is no strange thought to the reader of the Bible. New heavens and a new earth had been anticipated at least from the time that the Book of Isaiah was put together, and these new creations were expected to abide permanently (Isa. 65:17; 66:22). But John is more careful than the ancient prophet to make it clear that revelations of the new order are not just transformations of something old, but actually new creations. There are two words in the original Greek that mean "new"; one of them signifies that which is young in point of age, the other, that which is new in quality, fresh and unworn. It is this latter term that John uses here. Even as God "in the beginning" brought the heavens and earth into being out of chaos, so here, when all the earthly is destroyed he brings an entirely original world order to pass (compare II Peter 3:13). To the Jewish Christian of the early days it must have been comforting to read that "the sea was no more," both because of his dread of the literal sea and also because, as we have seen, the sea had come to stand for the worldliness of men's government that rolls its sweeping barrier between the dwellings of God's followers.

John sees not only a new heaven but also a new earth. Yet he immediately corrects any false impression this might leave by assuring his readers that the "new earth" is really made by a new city, not a city which has grown by process of social evolution from the earth up, but one which has come down from heaven as God's free gift to his redeemed (vs. 2). In his usual rapid change of figures, John not only sees the new order in terms of a new earth and a new city, but, as in 19:7-8, as a new bride, the bride of the Christ himself. In contrast with the wicked city "Babylon," the Rome of John's day, which was the harlot companion of her paramours (chs. 17-18), the joint figures of the beautiful city and the bride are sketched here for the joy of the saints' anticipation.

But the real purpose in picturing the new order as a city is to stress the thought of a group living together where it may be natural to realize that "the dwelling of God is with men" (vs. 3). Here is the longed-for renewal of the Garden of Eden. As in God's original fellowship with man he dwelt in the garden with him and talked with man and planned with him (Gen. 2:15-22), walking there with him "in the cool of the day" (Gen. 3:8), so here in this garden made new, God is "with them." And if we dwell in our thoughts upon the "idle tears they shed" when Adam and Eve were cast from their original home because of their sin, it is noteworthy that the author dwells lovingly, not only on God's being again with his people, but on his wiping away every tear and every reminder of the sting of death that had caused mourning and crying and pain (vs. 4). Even so the prophet of old had thought of a new age in which all tears would be wiped away (Isa. 25:8; compare Rev. 7:17). The presence of God brings no longer an expectation of judgment; it is the completely reassuring sign that the broken fellowship between heaven and earth is now restored. Paradise has been truly regained.

Man's New Life (21:5-8)

The renewed relationship results in newness of life. The words, "I make all things new" (vs. 5), are the fulfillment of the meaning of eternal life. And that eternal life can be completely realized because the God who is both "the beginning and the end" can say at last of his work, "It is done!" (vs. 6). The work of redemption, begun when man broke the first fellowship of Eden—begun, indeed, before that in the eternal purpose of God—is now perfected. Even as the dying Christ could exclaim on his triumphant cross, "It is finished" (John 19:30), so God the Father here says of all the work of redemption, "It is done!" It is especially thrilling to note John's reference to "the fountain of the water of life," since he had pictured as one of the most terrible of the results of judgment that the fountains had been turned to blood (16:4). In that scene of the judgment, the bowls of wrath, the last expiring breath of doom had been proclaimed when the seventh angel emptied his bowl upon the air and a great voice had uttered these same words, "It is done!" (16:17). What then was proclaimed in judgment is here uttered in mellow tones of triumph.

The new life is spoken of as the heritage of God's people and the new relationship as sonship to God (vs. 7). This is in the same vein of thought as that of Paul when he wrote of "the guarantee of our inheritance" (Eph. 1:14) and of "the spirit of sonship" which he said we had received in Christ (Rom. 8:15). Likewise, the author of the First Epistle of John had wistfully expressed the beautiful hope, "We are God's children now; it does not yet appear what we shall be, but we know that when he appears we shall be like him, for we shall see him as he is" (I John 3:2). The Book of Revelation, true to its lingering remembrance of the clouds of judgment, cannot leave such a wonderful picture of the new life of God's presence without contrasting the situation outside where those who have experienced the "second death" of separation from God must remain (vs. 8).

Detail of the New City (21:9-21)

The artistic sense of the apocalyptist revels in the delights of his vision. Even as he had not dared describe the harlot-city except from the "wilderness" (17:3), so he views the "holy city" from a mountaintop (vs. 10). The chief impression it made upon him was that of a radiant light which was the very glory of God (vs. 11). The first thesis of John's great epistle is that "God is light" (I John 1:5). Here the author of Revelation sees the fulfillment of that truth in the complete brilliance of the city where God dwells. Recalling the tent city before which Moses had caused the tribes of Israel to encamp three on each side (Num. 2), and the anticipation of the reconstructed city by Ezekiel (48:30-34), John describes the heavenly city as having three gates on each side set in "a great, high wall" (vss. 12-13). His sense of loyalty to his Hebrew heritage is seen in his vision of the names of the twelve tribes of Israel inscribed on the twelve gates (vs.

12). His unique faith as a Christian disciple is to be noted in his picture of the twelve foundations of the wall on which appeared the names of "the twelve apostles of the Lamb" (vs. 14). Thus it is that John emphasizes the unanimous view of early Christians that the Church was the successor of the ancient People of God. In the fact that both the gates and the foundations are twelve, the church number, can be seen an added emphasis on both the older and the newer people of God as his living Church.

The measurement of the new city (vss. 15-17) is in some respects an expansion of the earlier measuring of the Temple (11: 1-2). But the emphasis here on the great size of the city, twelve thousand stadia, or about fifteen hundred miles each way, reminds us once more of Ezekiel's measuring of the Temple area (Ezek. 42:16-20). In John's case the city is in the form of a cube, the ancient symbol of the perfect shape. The wall is measured in the apocalyptic number of the 144 cubits, the square of the church number, twelve (vs. 17), and the angel's measure is here mysteriously declared to be the same as a man's. The character of the new city appears in its being a solid cube of pure gold, a figure almost surpassing imagination (vs. 18). The foundations of the walls are pictured in terms of precious stones, most of which are probably not quite the equivalents of our modern stones of these names. That each one had some original symbolism is likely, though we should go far afield to discover it in each case. John has evidently been moved again by his remembrance of the stones in the resplendent breastplate of the high priest (Exod. 28: 15-21). Most wonderful of all is the inspired imagination which could picture the twelve gates of the city as made each of a single pearl. When we realize that John had dreamed of the wall in which these gates were set as being fifteen hundred miles high, his vision of the gates of single pearl is doubtless meant to say in a figure that the ways of God are past what we can even think!

Worship in the Holy City (21:22—22:5)

It is typical of the Book of Revelation that this climactic vision of the New Jerusalem should end with a scene of worship. Similarly, the main part of the book began with a double picture of the worship of the creator God and the redeeming Lamb (chs. 4-5). In the present sketch, though John introduces new and unique elements, he remains remarkably in harmony with the rest

of New Testament thought. Thus he startles his readers by presenting a heaven without a temple (vs. 22). One might expect
the very climax of apocalyptic thought to be in a rebuilt Temple,
even as Ezekiel's vision of the new age had been (Ezek. 40:1—
47:12). But to John's illumined eye the Lord God and the Lamb
of the earlier portion of his book become the very temple of worship. This reminds us of the revelation the Master made to the
woman of Sychar that the time would come when they would not
need to worship either in Samaria or in Jerusalem, giving as the
reason for this the fact that God is Spirit (John 4:21-24). It
blends also with the thought of another late New Testament
writer, "For Christ has entered, not into a sanctuary made with
hands, a copy of the true one, but into heaven itself" (Heb. 9:24).
So it is that John reiterates his belief that the city is one great
light, and he re-echoes his beautiful phrase "the glory of God"
(vs. 23) as descriptive of that light (see vs. 11), adding in the
mood of chapters 4-5 that "its lamp is the Lamb."

Some feel that there is an inconsistency in the writer's thought
that, "By its light shall the nations walk; and the kings of the
earth shall bring their glory into it" (vs. 24), since the nations
are supposed to have been totally destroyed and all kings but God
dethroned. But again, we are not dealing in Revelation with a
sequence of events, rather with a series of pictures which may be
viewed from many angles. The kings bringing their glory into
the city as well as the nations their honor (vs. 26), corresponds
in thought to the twenty-four elders casting their crowns before
the throne (4:10); it is another way of saying that the worship
they might have thought of receiving they now give to God. The
picture is one of a deep security, with the gates always open and
eternal day banishing the night of pillage (vs. 25). Both ideas, of
the nations bringing in their honor and of the gates open in peace,
found an earlier expression on a narrower scale in the prophet's
thought of the restoration of Israel (Isa. 60:3, 11).

For this writer, worship can never be far removed from the free
flowing of God's stream of truth, and so he reproduces (22:1)
another memorable vision of a prophet of the return of Israel—
that of "the river of the water of life." In the earlier concept
(Ezek. 47:1-12) this river flowed from under the rebuilt Temple;
here it issues from the very "throne of God and of the Lamb." In
the earlier instance the river flowed through the desert, nourish-
ing even the Dead Sea; in this instance it courses directly "through

the middle of the street of the city" (vs. 2). The stream is life-
giving, with its twelve kinds of fruit (the church number again)
appearing one each month and the leaves of its trees being "for
the healing of the nations." Again, literalism would get us into
trouble, for where are the nations that still need healing in the
city of complete redemption and why should healing be needed
when there is no more pain? But the follower of John's vision is
accustomed by this time to his freedom in using all kinds of figures that express his ecstatic thought.

The "water of life" is, of course, reminiscent of Jesus' further
words to the parched soul of the woman at Sychar's well (John
4:13-14) and of his words to the people of Jerusalem about the
rivers of water that spring up in the souls of believers (John 7:
37-38). The "tree of life" once more brings us back, with most
satisfying implications, to the story of the Garden of Eden. There,
after man had sinned by eating of the tree of knowledge, he was
banished from the Garden by the mercy of God lest he also eat
of the tree of life and become immortal in his sin (Gen. 3:22-24).
Now that redemption has been wrought, it is safe to eat of the
tree of life. Indeed, it is for the very purpose of leading men to
live that Jesus had come to bring God's salvation (John 10:10);
he had taught his disciples that "he who eats my flesh and drinks
my blood has eternal life" (John 6:54).

Another of this writer's daring reversals of the false dreams of
many is his insistence that heaven is no realm of idle pleasure but
of the union of service in praise: "his servants shall worship him"
(vs. 3). And still another, especially daring for the Jew, was that
men should come to see God's face (vs. 4). It had long been
understood that to look on the face of God was to invite death.
So Moses had been afraid to gaze on God even at the revelation
of the burning bush (Exod. 3:6). So, too, Isaiah had thought it
was woe to him that his eyes had seen the King before God
cleansed his innermost sin (Isa. 6:5-7). The Prologue to the
Fourth Gospel reminds us directly, "No one has ever seen God"
(John 1:18). But now, in the redemptive glory of the holy city,
even that barrier is removed, and God's servants may not only
behold his face but also wear the name of his ownership of
them right on their foreheads (vs. 4; compare 7:3). With a reiter-
ation of eternal light and of eternal rulership by God's entire
redeemed family, the vision of the new heaven and the new earth
comes to a glorious close.

CONCLUSION
Revelation 22:6-21

The last verses of Revelation contain a somewhat proverbial echoing of various gems of thought that have been typical of this book. There is the stress on truth that has so often characterized John's words (vs. 6). There is also the linkage of its thought with that of the prophets, for the God of the apocalyptist is also "the God of the spirits of the prophets." There is the repeated injunction, "I am coming soon" (vss. 7, 12, 20). We are reminded of the command of Jesus to his disciples when he was warning them of the impending destruction of Jerusalem and of his return, "Watch" (Mark 13:37). The coming of Christ to each individual, to each age, and to the whole world at its conclusion is rightly thought of as always just on the horizon. Only as one lives with the thought that he stands at any moment in the full presence of his Judge and Lord can he live with a consistent will. Here is also the renewed injunction to avoid the worship of any messenger of God, however grand, and to worship God alone (vss. 8-9), a warning given before to John by an angel (19:10).

Blessings and curses are mingled at the close of this book, as they have been all along. Perhaps the most terrible idea of God's eternal curse to be found anywhere in the Bible is here (vss. 10-11). These verses really go together, and it probably would be more in keeping with their thought if we rendered them, "For the time is near (when) the evildoer will still do evil, and the filthy still be filthy, and the righteous still do right, and the holy still be holy." It is the terrifying thought of an eternal state in which one is fixed by the life he has lived in the flesh and from which there is to be no further change. Redemption itself is completed. The time for salvation is passed. The curse is, of course, mingled with blessing, since the time is also gone when the righteous can lose his righteousness. This is indeed the bourne from which no traveler may return. The Judge-Redeemer represents himself to be coming, "bringing my recompense, to repay every one for what he has done" (vs. 12).

The other outstanding curse in this conclusion has to do with a kind of literary device, warning the reader not to tamper with anything in this book, either by adding to its words or taking from them (vss. 18-19). This refers, of course, simply to this last book

of the Bible, though it is a fitting warning for the total revelation of the Word of God. The strongest terms of the curse that
John can think of are that those who thus mutilate God's revealed
will to men will themselves find that their portion "in the tree of
life and in the holy city" is cut off.

But the blessings are more outstanding still. Two of the seven
beatitudes of this book have been saved for the conclusion.
"Blessed is he who keeps the words of the prophecy of this book"
(vs. 7). To "keep the words" is not to wrap them in a napkin and
bury them in the earth, nor yet simply to watch over them and
guard them from being stolen away, but rather to live them with
all the heart. The very last beatitude is pronounced upon the pure,
"those who wash their robes" (vs. 14). They have appeared before the throne much earlier in the vision (7:14). There they
were sealed and made safe from the beginning of all the cycles of
judgment, because they had "washed their robes and made them
white in the blood of the Lamb." Purity, along with truth, is the
outstanding quality of life that the apocalyptist looks for in the
redeemed. It is that which gives them ready access even to the
throne of the pure God himself. They have "the right to the tree
of life" and "may enter the city by the gates." In contrast,
there are named those impure who are kept outside the city (vs.
15), and it may not be too much to note that they are enumer-
ated by six different names, the number that is always that of man
without God, the number which falls short of the perfect seven.

This book also closes with a wondrous final invitation, in which
the redeeming Christ is joined by his redeemed Church. He is
spoken of as both "the root and the offspring of David" who had
been the redeemer of his people from their foes (vs. 16). He is
spoken of as "the bright morning star," that which reminds men
of the freshness of the new day. Through his "Spirit" and his
"Bride," that is, through the Holy Spirit and the Church, he issues
his glorious appeal to all men to come to him (vs. 17). Even on
the last page of the book, the apocalyptist is not so much inter-
ested in the "second coming" of Christ to men as he is in the first
coming of men to Christ. The book is definitely evangelistic. And
to link the Spirit and the Church in the appeal made from Christ
and on behalf of Christ is to place the most powerful form of
evangelism at the very close. Everyone who hears the appeal is
to add his own personal word, "Come." Everyone who is "thirsty"
is invited to come, and in John's view that would include all, for

there is no man outside of Christ but who thirsts for the water of life. But there is after all a limitation to the invitation. "Let him who desires take . . ." The more accurate rendering would be, "Let him who wills take . . ." This is a definite drawing of the line. Even the victorious and the ruling Christ will force no man. It is only the man who is willing who may come, even though Christ's water of life is "without price."

With a benediction of "the grace of the Lord Jesus" upon "all the saints" the final curtain is rung down on the greatest drama in all literature, the drama of God's redeeming power in Jesus Christ (vs. 21).

This book has contained nothing essentially new to the other portions of our New Testament. It proclaims the eternal message of salvation in ways that verify its claim to a place—in fact, the climactic place—in Holy Writ. True it is that certain of its emphases have been disturbing and to some extent unfamiliar. Its doctrine that the struggle within man between good and evil is the replica of an agelong conflict going on in the world order is magnificently conceived, even though unbelievable by many. That "good and evil" are never impersonal terms but always our earthly way of saying "God and the Devil" is the universal testimony of our New Testament. There is a dualism running through the Christian faith that will not be downed. It is the kind of dualism which makes sure that the difference between right and wrong is always significant. It is the kind that removes the least taint of evil intent from the purposes of God and places it where it belongs, on the selfish response of men to the Evil One. Revelation is consistent with the Christian message in its understanding that finite man would never be able of himself to concoct all the forms of evil to which flesh is heir. Evil exists somehow in the spirit world. That there is a Devil is the universal testimony of our New Testament. But that this Devil is never on a plane equal with God, that he is to have an end because he is always the loser in the long, long fight, is the encouragement that is also part of the gospel. This note of God's triumph is the assurance of his power to save and also of his power to destroy, not only the Devil himself but all those who persist in the ways of the Evil One. In the Book of Revelation, God's judgments are brought only slowly on the scene. They are only partial at the first, and they become final only when men refuse to repent.

If such a final view of judgment and salvation seems arbitrary and cold, let it be emphasized that in Revelation, as well as in the rest of the New Testament, the picture is placed against the background of God's great and eternal will to salvation. The same thoughts that reach their more refined expression in love and redemption as expressed in other volumes of our Bible, are by no means absent here. It must always be remembered that this book above all others pictures Christ as the Lamb. He is the Lamb that has been slain for our salvation, who has given his life that we may live.

It is true that the Christian life may be thought of as a spiritual conflict. There is a heavenly warfare which is unto the finish. No man, no nation, ever wins an earthly warfare. The only conflict that can ever be resolved is the conflict for the souls of men. We may engage as soldiers of God in this strife. And this warfare is conducted, not by a white horseman who brings the red and the black and the greenish-gray in his train, as the warrior of chapter 6, but by that White Horseman who is the Word of God, as he appears in chapter 19. The struggle by which God himself wins men from the Devil does not go on eternally; it has an issue, in which the Devil himself is thrown into the lake of fire. And that issue is determined by the Son of God himself. The final power of God's eternity is not alone, or chiefly, the power to destroy, but the power to save. The final winner in the conquest, bloody though it has been, is not a raging lion but the meek and lowly Lamb. The blood is not that of men or beasts shed in retaliation for the blood of martyrs, but the blood of sacrifice which the Lamb has been willing to shed. When the final field is won, it is the victory, not of a kingdom of force, but of a kingship whose symbol is forever a "Lamb standing, as though it had been slain."